William Shakespeare (bapt. 26 April 1564 – 23 April 1616) was an English poet, playwright and actor, widely regarded as the greatest writer in the English language and the world's greatest dramatist. He is often called England's national poet and the "Bard of Avon". His extant works, including collaborations, consist of approximately 39 plays, 154 sonnets, two long narrative poems, and a few other verses, some of uncertain authorship. His plays have been translated into every major living language and are performed more often than those of any other playwright. Shakespeare was born and raised in Stratford-upon-Avon, Warwickshire. At the age of 18, he married Anne Hathaway, with whom he had three children: Susanna and twins Hamnet and Judith. Sometime between 1585 and 1592, he began a successful career in London as an actor, writer, and part-owner of a playing company called the Lord Chamberlain's Men, later known as the King's Men. At age 49 (around 1613), he appears to have retired to Stratford, where he died three years later. (Source: Wikipedia)

Literary works:
The Tempest
The Two Gentlemen of Verona
The Merry Wives of Windsor
Measure for Measure
The Comedy of Errors
Much Ado About Nothing
Love's Labour's Lost
A Midsummer Night's Dream
The Merchant of Venice
As You Like It
The Taming of the Shrew
All's Well That Ends Well
Twelfth Night
The Winter's Tale
Pericles, Prince of Tyre
The Two Noble Kinsmen

TITUS ANDRONICUS
&
ROMEO AND JULIET
William Shakespeare

PRINCE CLASSICS

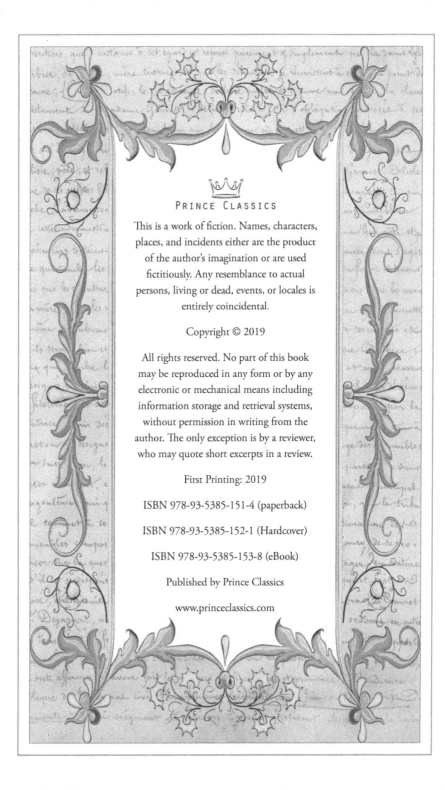

PRINCE CLASSICS

First Printing: 2019

ISBN 978-93-5385-151-4 (paperback)

ISBN 978-93-5385-152-1 (Hardcover)

ISBN 978-93-5385-153-8 (eBook)

Published by Prince Classics

www.princeclassics.com

Contents

TITUS ANDRONICUS
&
ROMEO AND JULIET

TITUS ANDRONICUS

PERSONS REPRESENTED.

SATURNINUS, Son to the late Emperor of Rome, afterwards declared Emperor.

BASSIANUS, Brother to Saturninus, in love with Lavinia.

TITUS ANDRONICUS, a noble Roman, General against the Goths.

MARCUS ANDRONICUS, Tribune of the People, and Brother to Titus.

LUCIUS, Son to Titus Andronicus.

QUINTUS, Son to Titus Andronicus.

MARTIUS, Son to Titus Andronicus.

MUTIUS, Son to Titus Andronicus.

YOUNG LUCIUS, a Boy, Son to Lucius.

PUBLIUS, Son to Marcus the Tribune.

AEMILIUS, a noble Roman.

ALARBUS, Son to Tamora.

DEMETRIUS, Son to Tamora.

CHIRON, Son to Tamora.

AARON, a Moor, beloved by Tamora

A Captain, Tribune, Messenger,and Clown—Romans

Goths and Romans.

TAMORA, Queen of the Goths

LAVINIA, Daughter to Titus Andronicus

A NURSE, and a black CHILD.

Kinsmen to Titus, Senators, Tribunes, Officers, Soldiers, and Attendants.

SCENE: Rome, and the Country near it.

ACT 1.

SCENE I. Rome. Before the Capitol.

[The Tomb of Andronic appearing; the Tribunes and Senators aloft.
Enter, below, SATURNINUS and his Followers on one side, and
BASSIANUS and his Followers at the other, with drums and colours.]

SATURNINUS.

Noble patricians, patrons of my right,

Defend the justice of my cause with arms;

And, countrymen, my loving followers,

Plead my successive title with your swords:

I am his first born son that was the last

That wore the imperial diadem of Rome:

Then let my father's honours live in me,

Nor wrong mine age with this indignity.

BASSIANUS.

Romans,—friends, followers, favourers of my right,—

If ever Bassianus, Caesar's son,

Were gracious in the eyes of royal Rome,

Keep then this passage to the Capitol;

And suffer not dishonour to approach

The imperial seat, to virtue consecrate,

To justice, continence, and nobility:

But let desert in pure election shine;

And, Romans, fight for freedom in your choice.

    [Enter MARCUS ANDRONICUS aloft, with the crown.]

MARCUS.

Princes,—that strive by factions and by friends

Ambitiously for rule and empery,—

Know that the people of Rome, for whom we stand

A special party, have by common voice,

In election for the Roman empery

Chosen Andronicus, surnamed Pius

For many good and great deserts to Rome:

A nobler man, a braver warrior,

Lives not this day within the city walls.:

He by the senate is accited home

From weary wars against the barbarous Goths;

That with his sons, a terror to our foes,

Hath yok'd a nation strong, train'd up in arms.

Ten years are spent since first he undertook

This cause of Rome, and chastised with arms

Our enemies' pride: five times he hath return'd

Bleeding to Rome, bearing his valiant sons

In coffins from the field;

And now at last, laden with honour's spoils,

Returns the good Andronicus to Rome,

Renowned Titus, flourishing in arms.

Let us entreat,—by honour of his name

Whom worthily you would have now succeed,

And in the Capitol and senate's right,

Whom you pretend to honour and adore,—

That you withdraw you and abate your strength;

Dismiss your followers, and, as suitors should,

Plead your deserts in peace and humbleness.

SATURNINUS.

How fair the tribune speaks to calm my thoughts!

BASSIANUS.

Marcus Andronicus, so I do affy

In thy uprightness and integrity,

And so I love and honour thee and thine,

Thy noble brother Titus and his sons,

And her to whom my thoughts are humbled all,

Gracious Lavinia, Rome's rich ornament,

That I will here dismiss my loving friends;

And to my fortunes and the people's favour

Commit my cause in balance to be weigh'd.

[Exeunt the Followers of BASSIANUS.]

SATURNINUS.

Friends, that have been thus forward in my right,

I thank you all and here dismiss you all;

And to the love and favour of my country

Commit myself, my person, and the cause.

[Exeunt the Followers of SATURNINUS.]

Rome, be as just and gracious unto me

As I am confident and kind to thee.—

Open the gates, tribunes, and let me in.

BASSIANUS.

Tribunes, and me, a poor competitor.

[Flourish. Exeunt; SATURNINUS and BASSIANUS go up into the
Capitol.]

[Enter a Captain.]

CAPTAIN.

Romans, make way. The good Andronicus,

Patron of virtue, Rome's best champion,

Successful in the battles that he fights,

With honour and with fortune is return'd

From where he circumscribed with his sword

And brought to yoke the enemies of Rome.

**[Flourish of trumpets, &c. Enter MARTIUS and MUTIUS; after
them two Men bearing a coffin covered with black; then LUCIUS and
QUINTUS. After them TITUS ANDRONICUS; and then TAMORA,
with ALARBUS, DEMETRIUS, CHIRON, AARON, and other Goths,
prisoners; soldiers and People following. The bearers set down the
coffin, and TITUS speaks.]**

TITUS.

Hail, Rome, victorious in thy mourning weeds!

Lo, as the bark that hath discharg'd her fraught

Returns with precious lading to the bay

From whence at first she weigh'd her anchorage,

Cometh Andronicus, bound with laurel boughs,

To re-salute his country with his tears,—

Tears of true joy for his return to Rome.—

Thou great defender of this Capitol,

Stand gracious to the rites that we intend!—

Romans, of five and twenty valiant sons,

Half of the number that King Priam had,

Behold the poor remains, alive and dead!

These that survive let Rome reward with love;

These that I bring unto their latest home,

With burial amongst their ancestors;

Here Goths have given me leave to sheathe my sword.

Titus, unkind, and careless of thine own,

Why suffer'st thou thy sons, unburied yet,

To hover on the dreadful shore of Styx?—

Make way to lay them by their brethren.—

[The tomb is opened.]

There greet in silence, as the dead are wont,

And sleep in peace, slain in your country's wars!

O sacred receptacle of my joys,

Sweet cell of virtue and nobility,

How many sons of mine hast thou in store,

That thou wilt never render to me more!

LUCIUS.

Give us the proudest prisoner of the Goths,

That we may hew his limbs, and on a pile

Ad manes fratrum sacrifice his flesh

Before this earthy prison of their bones;

That so the shadows be not unappeas'd,

Nor we disturb'd with prodigies on earth.

TITUS.

I give him you,—the noblest that survives,

The eldest son of this distressed queen.

TAMORA.

Stay, Roman brethen!—Gracious conqueror,

Victorious Titus, rue the tears I shed,

A mother's tears in passion for her son:

And if thy sons were ever dear to thee,

O, think my son to be as dear to me!

Sufficeth not that we are brought to Rome,

To beautify thy triumphs and return,

Captive to thee and to thy Roman yoke;

But must my sons be slaughter'd in the streets

For valiant doings in their country's cause?

O, if to fight for king and common weal

Were piety in thine, it is in these.

Andronicus, stain not thy tomb with blood:

Wilt thou draw near the nature of the gods?

Draw near them, then, in being merciful:

Sweet mercy is nobility's true badge:

Thrice-noble Titus, spare my first-born son.

TITUS.

Patient yourself, madam, and pardon me.

These are their brethren, whom your Goths beheld

Alive and dead; and for their brethren slain

Religiously they ask a sacrifice:

To this your son is mark'd; and die he must,

To appease their groaning shadows that are gone.

LUCIUS.

Away with him! and make a fire straight;

And with our swords, upon a pile of wood,

Let's hew his limbs till they be clean consum'd.

> [Exeunt LUCIUS, QUINTUS, MARTIUS, and MUTIUS with
> ALARBUS.]

TAMORA.

O cruel, irreligious piety!

CHIRON.

Was ever Scythia half so barbarous!

DEMETRIUS.

Oppose not Scythia to ambitious Rome.

Alarbus goes to rest; and we survive

To tremble under Titus' threatening look.

Then, madam, stand resolv'd; but hope withal

The self-same gods that arm'd the Queen of Troy

With opportunity of sharp revenge

Upon the Thracian tyrant in his tent,

May favour Tamora, the queen of Goths,—

When Goths were Goths and Tamora was queen,—

To quit the bloody wrongs upon her foes.

[Re-enter LUCIUS, QUINTUS, MARTIUS,and MUTIUS, with their swords bloody.]

LUCIUS.

See, lord and father, how we have perform'd

Our Roman rites: Alarbus' limbs are lopp'd,

And entrails feed the sacrificing fire,

Whose smoke like incense doth perfume the sky.

Remaineth naught but to inter our brethren,

And with loud 'larums welcome them to Rome.

TITUS.

Let it be so, and let Andronicus

Make this his latest farewell to their souls.

[Trumpets sounded and the coffin laid in the tomb.]

In peace and honour rest you here, my sons;

Rome's readiest champions, repose you here in rest,

Secure from worldly chances and mishaps!

Here lurks no treason, here no envy swells,

Here grow no damned grudges; here are no storms,

No noise, but silence and eternal sleep:

[Enter LAVINIA.]

In peace and honour rest you here, my sons!

LAVINIA.

In peace and honour live Lord Titus long;

My noble lord and father, live in fame!

Lo, at this tomb my tributary tears

I render for my brethren's obsequies;

And at thy feet I kneel, with tears of joy

Shed on this earth for thy return to Rome;

O, bless me here with thy victorious hand,

Whose fortunes Rome's best citizens applaud!

TITUS.

Kind Rome, that hast thus lovingly reserv'd

The cordial of mine age to glad my heart!—

Lavinia, live; outlive thy father's days,

And fame's eternal date, for virtue's praise!

[Enter, below, MARCUS ANDRONICUS and Tribunes; re-enter

SATURNINUS, BASSIANUS, and Attendants.]

MARCUS.

Long live Lord Titus, my beloved brother,

Gracious triumpher in the eyes of Rome!

TITUS.

Thanks, gentle tribune, noble brother Marcus.

MARCUS.

And welcome, nephews, from successful wars,

You that survive and you that sleep in fame!

Fair lords, your fortunes are alike in all,

That in your country's service drew your swords:

But safer triumph is this funeral pomp

That hath aspir'd to Solon's happiness

And triumphs over chance in honour's bed.—

Titus Andronicus, the people of Rome,

Whose friend in justice thou hast ever been,

Send thee by me, their tribune and their trust,

This palliament of white and spotless hue;

And name thee in election for the empire

With these our late-deceased emperor's sons:

Be candidatus then, and put it on,

And help to set a head on headless Rome.

TITUS.

A better head her glorious body fits

Than his that shakes for age and feebleness:

What, should I don this robe and trouble you?

Be chosen with proclamations to-day,

To-morrow yield up rule, resign my life,

And set abroach new business for you all?

Rome, I have been thy soldier forty years,

And led my country's strength successfully,

And buried one-and-twenty valiant sons,

Knighted in field, slain manfully in arms,

In right and service of their noble country:

Give me a staff of honour for mine age,

But not a sceptre to control the world;

Upright he held it, lords, that held it last.

MARCUS.

Titus, thou shalt obtain and ask the empery.

SATURNINUS.

Proud and ambitious tribune, canst thou tell?

TITUS.

Patience, Prince Saturninus.

SATURNINUS.

Romans, do me right;—

Patricians, draw your swords, and sheathe them not

Till Saturninus be Rome's Emperor.—

Andronicus, would thou were shipp'd to hell

Rather than rob me of the people's hearts!

LUCIUS.

Proud Saturnine, interrupter of the good

That noble-minded Titus means to thee!

TITUS.

Content thee, prince; I will restore to thee

The people's hearts, and wean them from themselves.

BASSIANUS.

Andronicus, I do not flatter thee,

But honour thee, and will do till I die.

My faction if thou strengthen with thy friends,

I will most thankful be; and thanks to men

Of noble minds is honourable meed.

TITUS.

People of Rome, and people's tribunes here,

I ask your voices and your suffrages:

Will you bestow them friendly on Andronicus?

TRIBUNES.

To gratify the good Andronicus,

And gratulate his safe return to Rome,

The people will accept whom he admits.

TITUS.

Tribunes, I thank you: and this suit I make,

That you create your emperor's eldest son,

Lord Saturnine; whose virtues will, I hope,

Reflect on Rome as Titan's rays on earth,

And ripen justice in this commonweal:

Then, if you will elect by my advice,

Crown him, and say 'Long live our Emperor!'

MARCUS.

With voices and applause of every sort,

Patricians and plebeians, we create

Lord Saturninus Rome's great emperor;

And say 'Long live our Emperor Saturnine!'

[A long flourish.]

SATURNINUS.

Titus Andronicus, for thy favours done

To us in our election this day

I give thee thanks in part of thy deserts,

And will with deeds requite thy gentleness;

And for an onset, Titus, to advance

Thy name and honourable family,

Lavinia will I make my empress,

Rome's royal mistress, mistress of my heart,

And in the sacred Pantheon her espouse:

Tell me, Andronicus, doth this motion please thee?

TITUS.

It doth, my worthy lord; and in this match

I hold me highly honoured of your grace:

And here in sight of Rome, to Saturnine,—

King and commander of our commonweal,

The wide world's emperor,—do I consecrate

My sword, my chariot, and my prisoners;

Presents well worthy Rome's imperious lord:

Receive them then, the tribute that I owe,

Mine honour's ensigns humbled at thy feet.

SATURNINUS.

Thanks, noble Titus, father of my life!

How proud I am of thee and of thy gifts

Rome shall record; and when I do forget

The least of these unspeakable deserts,

Romans, forget your fealty to me.

TITUS.

[To TAMORA.] Now, madam, are you prisoner to an emperor;

To him that for your honour and your state

Will use you nobly and your followers.

SATURNINUS.

A goodly lady, trust me; of the hue

That I would choose, were I to choose anew.—

Clear up, fair queen, that cloudy countenance:

Though chance of war hath wrought this change of cheer,

Thou com'st not to be made a scorn in Rome:

Princely shall be thy usage every way.

Rest on my word, and let not discontent

Daunt all your hopes: madam, he comforts you

Can make you greater than the Queen of Goths.—

Lavinia, you are not displeas'd with this?

LAVINIA.

Not I, my lord, sith true nobility

Warrants these words in princely courtesy.

SATURNINUS.

Thanks, sweet Lavinia.—Romans, let us go:

Ransomless here we set our prisoners free:

Proclaim our honours, lords, with trump and drum.

[Flourish. SATURNINUS courts TAMORA in dumb show.]

BASSIANUS.

Lord Titus, by your leave, this maid is mine.

[Seizing LAVINIA.]

TITUS.

How, sir! are you in earnest then, my lord?

BASSIANUS.

Ay, noble Titus; and resolv'd withal

27

To do myself this reason and this right.

MARCUS.

Suum cuique is our Roman justice:

This prince in justice seizeth but his own.

LUCIUS.

And that he will and shall, if Lucius live.

TITUS.

Traitors, avaunt!—Where is the emperor's guard?—

Treason, my lord,—Lavinia is surpris'd!

SATURNINUS.

Surpris'd! by whom?

BASSIANUS.

By him that justly may

Bear his betroth'd from all the world away.

[Exeunt BASSIANUS and MARCUS with LAVINIA.]

MUTIUS.

Brothers, help to convey her hence away,

And with my sword I'll keep this door safe.

[Exeunt LUCIUS, QUINTUS, and MARTIUS.]

TITUS.

Follow, my lord, and I'll soon bring her back.

MUTIUS.

My lord, you pass not here.

TITUS.

What, villain boy!

Barr'st me my way in Rome?

[Stabbing MUTIUS.]

MUTIUS.

Help, Lucius, help!

[Dies.]

[Re-enter Lucius.]

LUCIUS.

My lord, you are unjust; and more than so:

In wrongful quarrel you have slain your son.

TITUS.

Nor thou nor he are any sons of mine;

My sons would never so dishonour me.

Traitor, restore Lavinia to the Emperor.

LUCIUS.

Dead, if you will; but not to be his wife,

That is another's lawful promis'd love.

[Exit.]

SATURNINUS.

No, Titus, no; the emperor needs her not,

Nor her, nor thee, nor any of thy stock:

I'll trust by leisure him that mocks me once;

Thee never, nor thy traitorous haughty sons,

Confederates all thus to dishonour me.

Was there none else in Rome to make a stale

But Saturnine? Full well, Andronicus,

Agree these deeds with that proud brag of thine

That said'st I begg'd the empire at thy hands.

TITUS.

O monstrous! what reproachful words are these?

SATURNINUS.

But go thy ways; go, give that changing piece

To him that flourish'd for her with his sword;

A valiant son-in-law thou shalt enjoy;

One fit to bandy with thy lawless sons,

To ruffle in the commonwealth of Rome.

TITUS.

These words are razors to my wounded heart.

SATURNINUS.

And therefore, lovely Tamora, Queen of Goths,—

That, like the stately Phoebe 'mongst her nymphs,

Dost overshine the gallant'st dames of Rome,—

If thou be pleas'd with this my sudden choice,

Behold, I choose thee, Tamora, for my bride

And will create thee empress of Rome.

Speak, Queen of Goths, dost thou applaud my choice?

And here I swear by all the Roman gods,—

Sith priest and holy water are so near,

And tapers burn so bright, and everything

In readiness for Hymenaeus stand,—

I will not re-salute the streets of Rome,

Or climb my palace, till from forth this place

I lead espous'd my bride along with me.

TAMORA.

And here in sight of heaven to Rome I swear,

If Saturnine advance the Queen of Goths,

She will a handmaid be to his desires,

A loving nurse, a mother to his youth.

SATURNINUS.

Ascend, fair queen, Pantheon.—Lords, accompany

Your noble emperor and his lovely bride,

Sent by the heavens for Prince Saturnine,

Whose wisdom hath her fortune conquered:

There shall we consummate our spousal rites.

[Exeunt SATURNINUS and his Followers; TAMORA and her Sons; AARON and Goths.]

TITUS.

I am not bid to wait upon this bride.—

Titus, when wert thou wont to walk alone,

Dishonour'd thus, and challenged of wrongs?

[Re-enter MARCUS, LUCIUS, QUINTUS, and MARTIUS.]

MARCUS.

O Titus, see, O, see what thou hast done!

In a bad quarrel slain a virtuous son.

TITUS.

No, foolish tribune, no; no son of mine,—

Nor thou, nor these, confederates in the deed

That hath dishonoured all our family;

Unworthy brother and unworthy sons!

LUCIUS.

But let us give him burial, as becomes;

Give Mutius burial with our bretheren.

TITUS.

Traitors, away! He rests not in this tomb:—

This monument five hundred years hath stood,

Which I have sumptuously re-edified:

Here none but soldiers and Rome's servitors

Repose in fame; none basely slain in brawls:—

Bury him where you can, he comes not here.

MARCUS.

My lord, this is impiety in you:

My nephew Mutius' deeds do plead for him;

He must be buried with his bretheren.

QUINTUS & MARTIUS.

And shall, or him we will accompany.

TITUS.

And shall! What villain was it spake that word?

QUINTUS.

He that would vouch it in any place but here.

TITUS.

What, would you bury him in my despite?

MARCUS.

No, noble Titus; but entreat of thee

To pardon Mutius, and to bury him.

TITUS.

Marcus, even thou hast struck upon my crest,

And with these boys mine honour thou hast wounded:

My foes I do repute you every one;

So trouble me no more, but get you gone.

MARTIUS.

He is not with himself; let us withdraw.

QUINTUS.

Not I, till Mutius' bones be buried.

       [MARCUS and the Sons of TITUS kneel.]

MARCUS.

Brother, for in that name doth nature plead,—

QUINTUS.

Father, and in that name doth nature speak,—

TITUS.

Speak thou no more, if all the rest will speed.

MARCUS.

Renowned Titus, more than half my soul,—

LUCIUS.

Dear father, soul and substance of us all,—

MARCUS.

Suffer thy brother Marcus to inter

His noble nephew here in virtue's nest,

That died in honour and Lavinia's cause:

Thou art a Roman,—be not barbarous.

The Greeks upon advice did bury Ajax,

That slew himself; and wise Laertes' son

Did graciously plead for his funerals:

Let not young Mutius, then, that was thy joy,

Be barr'd his entrance here.

TITUS.

Rise, Marcus, rise:

The dismall'st day is this that e'er I saw,

To be dishonour'd by my sons in Rome!—

Well, bury him, and bury me the next.

[MUTIUS is put into the tomb.]

LUCIUS.

There lie thy bones, sweet Mutius, with thy friends,

Till we with trophies do adorn thy tomb.

ALL.

[Kneeling.] No man shed tears for noble Mutius;

He lives in fame that died in virtue's cause.

MARCUS.

My lord,—to step out of these dreary dumps,—

How comes it that the subtle Queen of Goths

Is of a sudden thus advanc'd in Rome?

TITUS.

I know not, Marcus, but I know it is,—

Whether by device or no, the heavens can tell:

Is she not, then, beholding to the man

That brought her for this high good turn so far?

MARCUS.

Yes, and will nobly him remunerate.

**[Flourish. Re-enter, at one side, SATURNINUS, attended; TAMORA
DEMETRIUS, CHIRON, and AARON; at the other, BASSIANUS,
LAVINIA, and others.]**

SATURNINUS.

So, Bassianus, you have play'd your prize:

God give you joy, sir, of your gallant bride!

BASSIANUS.

And you of yours, my lord! I say no more,

Nor wish no less; and so I take my leave.

SATURNINUS.

Traitor, if Rome have law or we have power,

Thou and thy faction shall repent this rape.

BASSIANUS.

Rape, call you it, my lord, to seize my own,

My true betrothed love, and now my wife?

But let the laws of Rome determine all;

Meanwhile am I possess'd of that is mine.

SATURNINUS.

'Tis good, sir. You are very short with us;

But if we live we'll be as sharp with you.

BASSIANUS.

My lord, what I have done, as best I may,

Answer I must, and shall do with my life.

Only thus much I give your grace to know,—

By all the duties that I owe to Rome,

This noble gentleman, Lord Titus here,

Is in opinion and in honour wrong'd,

That, in the rescue of Lavinia,

With his own hand did slay his youngest son,

In zeal to you, and highly mov'd to wrath

To be controll'd in that he frankly gave:

Receive him then to favour, Saturnine,

That hath express'd himself in all his deeds

A father and a friend to thee and Rome.

TITUS.

Prince Bassianus, leave to plead my deeds:

'Tis thou and those that have dishonour'd me.

Rome and the righteous heavens be my judge

How I have lov'd and honour'd Saturnine!

TAMORA.

My worthy lord, if ever Tamora

Were gracious in those princely eyes of thine,

Then hear me speak indifferently for all;

And at my suit, sweet, pardon what is past.

SATURNINUS.

What, madam! be dishonoured openly,

And basely put it up without revenge?

TAMORA.

Not so, my lord; the gods of Rome forfend

I should be author to dishonour you!

But on mine honour dare I undertake

For good Lord Titus' innocence in all,

Whose fury not dissembled speaks his griefs:

Then at my suit look graciously on him;

Lose not so noble a friend on vain suppose,

Nor with sour looks afflict his gentle heart.—

[Aside.] My lord, be rul'd by me, be won at last;

Dissemble all your griefs and discontents:

You are but newly planted in your throne;

Lest, then, the people, and patricians too,

Upon a just survey take Titus' part,

And so supplant you for ingratitude,—

Which Rome reputes to be a heinous sin,—

Yield at entreats; and then let me alone:

I'll find a day to massacre them all,

And raze their faction and their family,

The cruel father and his traitorous sons,

To whom I sued for my dear son's life;

And make them know what 'tis to let a queen

Kneel in the streets and beg for grace in vain.—

Come, come, sweet emperor,—come, Andronicus,—

Take up this good old man, and cheer the heart

That dies in tempest of thy angry frown.

SATURNINUS.

Rise, Titus, rise; my empress hath prevail'd.

TITUS.

I thank your majesty and her, my lord:

These words, these looks, infuse new life in me.

TAMORA.

Titus, I am incorporate in Rome,

A Roman now adopted happily,

And must advise the emperor for his good.

This day all quarrels die, Andronicus;—

And let it be mine honour, good my lord,

That I have reconcil'd your friends and you. —

For you, Prince Bassianus, I have pass'd

My word and promise to the emperor

That you will be more mild and tractable.—

And fear not, lords,—and you, Lavinia,—

By my advice, all humbled on your knees,

You shall ask pardon of his majesty.

LUCIUS.

We do; and vow to heaven and to his highness

That what we did was mildly as we might,

Tendering our sister's honour and our own.

MARCUS.

That on mine honour here do I protest.

SATURNINUS.

Away, and talk not; trouble us no more.

TAMORA.

Nay, nay, sweet emperor, we must all be friends:

The tribune and his nephews kneel for grace;

I will not be denied: sweet heart, look back.

SATURNINUS.

Marcus, for thy sake, and thy brother's here,

And at my lovely Tamora's entreats,

I do remit these young men's heinous faults:

Stand up.—

Lavinia, though you left me like a churl,

I found a friend; and sure as death I swore

I would not part a bachelor from the priest.

Come, if the emperor's court can feast two brides,

You are my guest, Lavinia, and your friends.

This day shall be a love-day, Tamora.

TITUS.

To-morrow, an it please your majesty

To hunt the panther and the hart with me,

With horn and hound we'll give your grace bonjour.

SATURNINUS.

Be it so, Titus, and gramercy too.

[Exeunt.]

ACT II.

SCENE I. Rome. Before the palace.

[Enter AARON.]

AARON.

Now climbeth Tamora Olympus' top,

Safe out of fortune's shot; and sits aloft,

Secure of thunder's crack or lightning's flash;

Advanc'd above pale envy's threatening reach.

As when the golden sun salutes the morn,

And, having gilt the ocean with his beams,

Gallops the zodiac in his glistening coach,

And overlooks the highest-peering hill;

So Tamora:

Upon her wit doth earthly honour wait,

And virtue stoops and trembles at her frown.

Then, Aaron, arm thy heart and fit thy thoughts

To mount aloft with thy imperial mistress,

And mount her pitch, whom thou in triumph long

Hast prisoner held, fett'red in amorous chains,

And faster bound to Aaron's charming eyes

Than is Prometheus tied to Caucasus.

Away with slavish weeds and servile thoughts!

I will be bright, and shine in pearl and gold,

To wait upon this new-made empress.

To wait, said I? to wanton with this queen,

This goddess, this Semiramis, this nymph,

This siren, that will charm Rome's Saturnine,

And see his shipwreck and his commonweal's.—

Holla! what storm is this?

[**Enter DEMETRIUS and CHIRON braving.**]

DEMETRIUS.

Chiron, thy years wants wit, thy wit wants edge

And manners, to intrude where I am grac'd;

And may, for aught thou know'st, affected be.

CHIRON.

Demetrius, thou dost over-ween in all;

And so in this, to bear me down with braves.

'Tis not the difference of a year or two

Makes me less gracious or thee more fortunate:

I am as able and as fit as thou

To serve and to deserve my mistress' grace;

And that my sword upon thee shall approve,

And plead my passions for Lavinia's love.

AARON.

[Aside.] Clubs, clubs! These lovers will not keep the peace.

DEMETRIUS.

Why, boy, although our mother, unadvis'd,

Gave you a dancing-rapier by your side,

Are you so desperate grown to threat your friends?

Go to; have your lath glu'd within your sheath

Till you know better how to handle it.

CHIRON.

Meanwhile, sir, with the little skill I have,

Full well shalt thou perceive how much I dare.

DEMETRIUS.

Ay, boy, grow ye so brave?

[They draw.]

AARON.

[Coming forward.] Why, how now, lords!

So near the emperor's palace dare ye draw,

And maintain such a quarrel openly?

Full well I wot the ground of all this grudge:

I would not for a million of gold

The cause were known to them it most concerns;

Nor would your noble mother for much more

Be so dishonour'd in the court of Rome.

For shame, put up.

DEMETRIUS.

Not I, till I have sheath'd

My rapier in his bosom, and withal

Thrust those reproachful speeches down his throat

That he hath breath'd in my dishonour here.

CHIRON.

For that I am prepar'd and full resolv'd,—

Foul-spoken coward, that thunder'st with thy tongue,

And with thy weapon nothing dar'st perform.

AARON.

Away, I say!—

Now, by the gods that warlike Goths adore,

This pretty brabble will undo us all.—

Why, lords, and think you not how dangerous

It is to jet upon a prince's right?

What, is Lavinia then become so loose,

Or Bassianus so degenerate,

That for her love such quarrels may be broach'd

Without controlment, justice, or revenge?

Young lords, beware! and should the empress know

This discord's ground, the music would not please.

CHIRON.

I care not, I, knew she and all the world:

I love Lavinia more than all the world.

DEMETRIUS.

Youngling, learn thou to make some meaner choice:

Lavina is thine elder brother's hope.

AARON.

Why, are ye mad? or know ye not in Rome

How furious and impatient they be,

And cannot brook competitors in love?

I tell you, lords, you do but plot your deaths

By this device.

CHIRON.

Aaron, a thousand deaths

Would I propose to achieve her whom I love.

AARON.

To achieve her!—How?

DEMETRIUS.

Why mak'st thou it so strange?

She is a woman, therefore may be woo'd;

She is a woman, therefore may be won;

She is Lavinia, therefore must be lov'd.

What, man! more water glideth by the mill

Than wots the miller of; and easy it is

Of a cut loaf to steal a shive, we know:

Though Bassianus be the emperor's brother,

Better than he have worn Vulcan's badge.

AARON.

[Aside.] Ay, and as good as Saturninus may.

DEMETRIUS.

Then why should he despair that knows to court it

With words, fair looks, and liberality?

What, hast not thou full often struck a doe,

And borne her cleanly by the keeper's nose?

AARON.

Why, then, it seems some certain snatch or so

Would serve your turns.

CHIRON.

Ay, so the turn were serv'd.

DEMETRIUS.

Aaron, thou hast hit it.

AARON.

Would you had hit it too!

Then should not we be tir'd with this ado.

Why, hark ye, hark ye,—and are you such fools

To square for this? Would it offend you, then,

That both should speed?

CHIRON.

Faith, not me.

DEMETRIUS.

Nor me, so I were one.

AARON.

For shame, be friends, and join for that you jar:

'Tis policy and stratagem must do

That you affect; and so must you resolve

That what you cannot as you would achieve,

You must perforce accomplish as you may.

Take this of me,—Lucrece was not more chaste

Than this Lavinia, Bassianus' love.

A speedier course than lingering languishment

Must we pursue, and I have found the path.

My lords, a solemn hunting is in hand;

There will the lovely Roman ladies troop:

The forest walks are wide and spacious;

And many unfrequented plots there are

Fitted by kind for rape and villainy:

Single you thither, then, this dainty doe,

And strike her home by force if not by words:

This way, or not at all, stand you in hope.

Come, come, our empress, with her sacred wit

To villainy and vengeance consecrate,

Will we acquaint with all what we intend;

And she shall file our engines with advice

That will not suffer you to square yourselves,

But to your wishes' height advance you both.

The emperor's court is like the house of fame,

The palace full of tongues, of eyes, and ears:

The woods are ruthless, dreadful, deaf, and dull;

There speak and strike, brave boys, and take your turns;

There serve your lust, shadowed from heaven's eye,

And revel in Lavinia's treasury.

CHIRON.

Thy counsel, lad, smells of no cowardice.

DEMETRIUS.

Sit fas aut nefas, till I find the stream

To cool this heat, a charm to calm these fits,

Per Styga, per manes vehor.

[Exeunt.]

SCENE II. A Forest near Rome; a Lodge seen at a distance. Horns and cry of hounds heard.

[Enter TITUS ANDRONICUS, with hunters, &c., MARCUS, LUCIUS, QUINTUS, and MARTIUS.]

TITUS.

The hunt is up, the morn is bright and gay,

The fields are fragrant, and the woods are green.

Uncouple here, and let us make a bay,

And wake the emperor and his lovely bride,

And rouse the prince, and ring a hunter's peal,

That all the court may echo with the noise.

Sons, let it be your charge, as it is ours,

To attend the emperor's person carefully:

I have been troubled in my sleep this night,

But dawning day new comfort hath inspir'd.

[Horns in a peal. Enter SATURNINUS, TAMORA, BASSIANUS, LAVINIA, DEMETRIUS, CHIRON, and Attendants.]

Many good morrows to your majesty:—

Madam, to you as many and as good:—

I promised your grace a hunter's peal.

SATURNINUS.

And you have rung it lustily, my lord;

Somewhat too early for new-married ladies.

BASSIANUS.

Lavinia, how say you?

LAVINIA.

I say no; I have been broad awake two hours and more.

SATURNINUS.

Come on then, horse and chariots let us have,

And to our sport.—[To TAMORA.] Madam, now shall ye see

Our Roman hunting.

MARCUS.

I have dogs, my lord,

Will rouse the proudest panther in the chase,

And climb the highest promontory top.

TITUS.

And I have horse will follow where the game

Makes way, and run like swallows o'er the plain.

DEMETRIUS.

Chiron, we hunt not, we, with horse nor hound,

But hope to pluck a dainty doe to ground.

[Exeunt.]

SCENE III. A lonely part of the Forest.

[Enter AARON with a bag of gold.]

AARON.

He that had wit would think that I had none,

To bury so much gold under a tree,

And never after to inherit it.

Let him that thinks of me so abjectly

Know that this gold must coin a stratagem,

Which, cunningly effected, will beget

A very excellent piece of villainy:

And so repose, sweet gold, for their unrest

[Hides the gold.]

That have their alms out of the empress' chest.

[Enter TAMORA.]

TAMORA.

My lovely Aaron, wherefore look'st thou sad

When everything does make a gleeful boast?

The birds chant melody on every bush;

The snakes lie rolled in the cheerful sun;

The green leaves quiver with the cooling wind,

And make a chequer'd shadow on the ground:

Under their sweet shade, Aaron, let us sit,

And whilst the babbling echo mocks the hounds,

Replying shrilly to the well-tun'd horns,

As if a double hunt were heard at once,

Let us sit down and mark their yelping noise;

And,—after conflict such as was suppos'd

The wandering prince and Dido once enjoy'd,

When with a happy storm they were surpris'd,

And curtain'd with a counsel-keeping cave,—

We may, each wreathed in the other's arms,

Our pastimes done, possess a golden slumber;

Whiles hounds and horns and sweet melodious birds

Be unto us as is a nurse's song

Of lullaby to bring her babe asleep.

AARON.

Madam, though Venus govern your desires,

Saturn is dominator over mine:

What signifies my deadly-standing eye,

My silence and my cloudy melancholy,

My fleece of woolly hair that now uncurls

Even as an adder when she doth unroll

To do some fatal execution?

No, madam, these are no venereal signs,

Vengeance is in my heart, death in my hand,

Blood and revenge are hammering in my head.

Hark, Tamora,—the empress of my soul,

Which never hopes more heaven than rests in thee,—

This is the day of doom for Bassianus;

His Philomel must lose her tongue to-day,

Thy sons make pillage of her chastity,

And wash their hands in Bassianus' blood.

Seest thou this letter? take it up, I pray thee,

And give the king this fatal-plotted scroll.—

Now question me no more,—we are espied;

Here comes a parcel of our hopeful booty,

Which dreads not yet their lives' destruction.

TAMORA.

Ah, my sweet Moor, sweeter to me than life!

AARON.

No more, great empress: Bassianus comes:

Be cross with him; and I'll go fetch thy sons

To back thy quarrels, whatsoe'er they be.

[Exit.]

[Enter BASSIANUS and LAVINIA.]

BASSIANUS.

Who have we here? Rome's royal empress,

Unfurnish'd of her well-beseeming troop?

Or is it Dian, habited like her,

Who hath abandoned her holy groves

To see the general hunting in this forest?

TAMORA.

Saucy controller of my private steps!

Had I the power that some say Dian had,

Thy temples should be planted presently

With horns, as was Actaeon's; and the hounds

Should drive upon thy new-transformed limbs,

Unmannerly intruder as thou art!

LAVINIA.

Under your patience, gentle empress,

'Tis thought you have a goodly gift in horning;

And to be doubted that your Moor and you

Are singled forth to try experiments;

Jove shield your husband from his hounds to-day!

'Tis pity they should take him for a stag.

BASSIANUS.

Believe me, queen, your swarth Cimmerian

Doth make your honour of his body's hue,

Spotted, detested, and abominable.

Why are you sequester'd from all your train,

Dismounted from your snow-white goodly steed,

And wander'd hither to an obscure plot,

Accompanied but with a barbarous Moor,

If foul desire had not conducted you?

LAVINIA.

And, being intercepted in your sport,

Great reason that my noble lord be rated

For sauciness.—I pray you let us hence,

And let her joy her raven-coloured love;

This valley fits the purpose passing well.

BASSIANUS.

The king my brother shall have notice of this.

LAVINIA.

Ay, for these slips have made him noted long:

Good king, to be so mightily abus'd!

TAMORA.

Why have I patience to endure all this?

[Enter DEMETRIUS and CHIRON.]

DEMETRIUS.

How now, dear sovereign, and our gracious mother!

Why doth your highness look so pale and wan?

TAMORA.

Have I not reason, think you, to look pale?

These two have 'ticed me hither to this place:—

A barren detested vale you see it is:

The trees, though summer, yet forlorn and lean,

O'ercome with moss and baleful mistletoe:

Here never shines the sun; here nothing breeds,

Unless the nightly owl or fatal raven:—

And when they show'd me this abhorred pit,

They told me, here, at dead time of the night,

A thousand fiends, a thousand hissing snakes,

Ten thousand swelling toads, as many urchins,

Would make such fearful and confused cries

As any mortal body hearing it

Should straight fall mad or else die suddenly.

No sooner had they told this hellish tale

But straight they told me they would bind me here

Unto the body of a dismal yew,

And leave me to this miserable death:

And then they call'd me foul adulteress,

Lascivious Goth, and all the bitterest terms

That ever ear did hear to such effect:

And had you not by wondrous fortune come,

This vengeance on me had they executed.

Revenge it, as you love your mother's life,

Or be ye not henceforth call'd my children.

DEMETRIUS.

This is a witness that I am thy son.

[Stabs BASSIANUS.]

CHIRON.

And this for me, struck home to show my strength.

[Also stabs BASSIANUS, who dies.]

LAVINIA.

Ay, come, Semiramis,—nay, barbarous Tamora,

For no name fits thy nature but thy own!

TAMORA.

Give me thy poniard;—you shall know, my boys,

Your mother's hand shall right your mother's wrong.

DEMETRIUS.

Stay, madam; here is more belongs to her;

First thrash the corn, then after burn the straw:

This minion stood upon her chastity,

Upon her nuptial vow, her loyalty,

And with that painted hope braves your mightiness:

And shall she carry this unto her grave?

CHIRON.

An if she do, I would I were an eunuch.

Drag hence her husband to some secret hole,

And make his dead trunk pillow to our lust.

TAMORA.

But when ye have the honey we desire,

Let not this wasp outlive, us both to sting.

CHIRON.

I warrant you, madam, we will make that sure.—

Come, mistress, now perforce we will enjoy

That nice-preserved honesty of yours.

LAVINIA.

O Tamora! thou bear'st a woman's face,—

TAMORA.

I will not hear her speak; away with her!

LAVINIA.

Sweet lords, entreat her hear me but a word.

DEMETRIUS.

Listen, fair madam: let it be your glory

To see her tears; but be your heart to them

As unrelenting flint to drops of rain.

LAVINIA.

When did the tiger's young ones teach the dam?

O, do not learn her wrath,—she taught it thee;

The milk thou suck'dst from her did turn to marble;

Even at thy teat thou hadst thy tyranny.—

Yet every mother breeds not sons alike:

[To CHIRON.] Do thou entreat her show a woman's pity.

CHIRON.

What, wouldst thou have me prove myself a bastard?

LAVINIA.

'Tis true, the raven doth not hatch a lark:

Yet have I heard,—O, could I find it now!—

The lion, mov'd with pity, did endure

To have his princely paws par'd all away.

Some say that ravens foster forlorn children,

The whilst their own birds famish in their nests:

O, be to me, though thy hard heart say no,

Nothing so kind, but something pitiful!

TAMORA.

I know not what it means:—away with her!

LAVINIA.

O, let me teach thee! for my father's sake,

That gave thee life, when well he might have slain thee,

Be not obdurate, open thy deaf ears.

TAMORA.

Hadst thou in person ne'er offended me,

Even for his sake am I pitiless.—

Remember, boys, I pour'd forth tears in vain

To save your brother from the sacrifice;

But fierce Andronicus would not relent:

Therefore away with her, and use her as you will;

The worse to her the better lov'd of me.

LAVINIA.

O Tamora, be call'd a gentle queen,

And with thine own hands kill me in this place!

For 'tis not life that I have begg'd so long;

Poor I was slain when Bassianus died.

TAMORA.

What begg'st thou, then? fond woman, let me go.

LAVINIA.

'Tis present death I beg; and one thing more,

That womanhood denies my tongue to tell:

O, keep me from their worse than killing lust,

And tumble me into some loathsome pit,

Where never man's eye may behold my body:

Do this, and be a charitable murderer.

TAMORA.

So should I rob my sweet sons of their fee:

No, let them satisfy their lust on thee.

DEMETRIUS.

Away! for thou hast stay'd us here too long.

LAVINIA.

No grace? no womanhood? Ah, beastly creature!

The blot and enemy to our general name!

Confusion fall,—

CHIRON.

Nay, then I'll stop your mouth:—bring thou her husband.

This is the hole where Aaron bid us hide him.

[DEMETRIUS throws BASSIANUS'S body into the pit; then exit
with CHIRON, dragging off LAVINIA.]

TAMORA.

Farewell, my sons: see that you make her sure:—

Ne'er let my heart know merry cheer indeed

Till all the Andronici be made away.

Now will I hence to seek my lovely Moor,

And let my spleenful sons this trull deflower.

[Exit.]

[Re-enter AARON, with QUINTUS and MARTIUS.]

AARON.

Come on, my lords, the better foot before:

Straight will I bring you to the loathsome pit

Where I espied the panther fast asleep.

QUINTUS.

My sight is very dull, whate'er it bodes.

MARTIUS.

And mine, I promise you; were't not for shame,

Well could I leave our sport to sleep awhile.

[Falls into the pit.]

QUINTUS.

What, art thou fallen?—What subtle hole is this,

Whose mouth is cover'd with rude-growing briers,

Upon whose leaves are drops of new-shed blood

As fresh as morning dew distill'd on flowers?

A very fatal place it seems to me.—

Speak, brother, hast thou hurt thee with the fall?

MARTIUS.

O brother, with the dismallest object hurt

That ever eye with sight made heart lament!

AARON.

[Aside] Now will I fetch the king to find them here,

That he thereby may have a likely guess

How these were they that made away his brother.

[Exit.]

MARTIUS.

Why dost not comfort me, and help me out

From this unhallow'd and blood-stained hole?

QUINTUS.

I am surprised with an uncouth fear;

A chilling sweat o'er-runs my trembling joints;

My heart suspects more than mine eye can see.

MARTIUS.

To prove thou hast a true divining heart,

Aaron and thou look down into this den,

And see a fearful sight of blood and death.

QUINTUS.

Aaron is gone; and my compassionate heart

Will not permit mine eyes once to behold

The thing whereat it trembles by surmise:

O, tell me who it is; for ne'er till now

Was I a child to fear I know not what.

MARTIUS.

Lord Bassianus lies embrewed here,

All on a heap, like to a slaughter'd lamb,

In this detested, dark, blood-drinking pit.

QUINTUS.

If it be dark, how dost thou know 'tis he?

MARTIUS.

Upon his bloody finger he doth wear

A precious ring that lightens all the hole,

Which, like a taper in some monument,

Doth shine upon the dead man's earthy cheeks,

And shows the ragged entrails of the pit:

So pale did shine the moon on Pyramus

When he by night lay bath'd in maiden blood.

O brother, help me with thy fainting hand,—

If fear hath made thee faint, as me it hath,—

Out of this fell devouring receptacle,

As hateful as Cocytus' misty mouth.

QUINTUS.

Reach me thy hand, that I may help thee out;

Or, wanting strength to do thee so much good,

I may be pluck'd into the swallowing womb

Of this deep pit, poor Bassianus' grave.

I have no strength to pluck thee to the brink.

MARTIUS.

Nor I no strength to climb without thy help.

QUINTUS.

Thy hand once more; I will not lose again,

Till thou art here aloft, or I below:

Thou canst not come to me,—I come to thee.

[Falls in.]

[Enter SATURNINUS with AARON.]

SATURNINUS.

Along with me: I'll see what hole is here,

And what he is that now is leap'd into it.—

Say, who art thou that lately didst descend

Into this gaping hollow of the earth?

MARTIUS.

The unhappy sons of old Andronicus,

Brought hither in a most unlucky hour,

To find thy brother Bassianus dead.

SATURNINUS.

My brother dead! I know thou dost but jest:

He and his lady both are at the lodge

Upon the north side of this pleasant chase;

'Tis not an hour since I left them there.

MARTIUS.

We know not where you left them all alive;

But, out, alas! here have we found him dead.

[Re-enter TAMORA, with Attendants; TITUS ANDRONICUS and LUCIUS.]

TAMORA.

Where is my lord the king?

SATURNINUS.

Here, Tamora; though griev'd with killing grief.

TAMORA.

Where is thy brother Bassianus?

SATURNINUS.

Now to the bottom dost thou search my wound;

Poor Bassianus here lies murdered.

TAMORA.

Then all too late I bring this fatal writ,

[Giving a letter.]

The complot of this timeless tragedy;

And wonder greatly that man's face can fold

In pleasing smiles such murderous tyranny.

65

SATURNINUS.

[Reads] 'An if we miss to meet him handsomely,—

Sweet huntsman, Bassianus 'tis we mean,—

Do thou so much as dig the grave for him:

Thou know'st our meaning. Look for thy reward

Among the nettles at the elder-tree

Which overshades the mouth of that same pit

Where we decreed to bury Bassianus.

Do this, and purchase us thy lasting friends.'

O Tamora! was ever heard the like?—

This is the pit and this the elder-tree:—

Look, sirs, if you can find the huntsman out

That should have murder'd Bassianus here.

AARON.

My gracious lord, here is the bag of gold.

[Showing it.]

SATURNINUS.

[To TITUS] Two of thy whelps, fell curs of bloody kind,

Have here bereft my brother of his life.—

Sirs, drag them from the pit unto the prison:

There let them bide until we have devis'd

Some never-heard-of torturing pain for them.

TAMORA.

What, are they in this pit? O wondrous thing!

How easily murder is discovered!

TITUS.

High emperor, upon my feeble knee

I beg this boon, with tears not lightly shed,

That this fell fault of my accursed sons,—

Accursed if the fault be prov'd in them,—

SATURNINUS.

If it be prov'd! You see it is apparent.—

Who found this letter? Tamora, was it you?

TAMORA.

Andronicus himself did take it up.

TITUS.

I did, my lord: yet let me be their bail;

For, by my fathers' reverend tomb, I vow

They shall be ready at your highness' will

To answer their suspicion with their lives.

SATURNINUS.

Thou shalt not bail them: see thou follow me.—

Some bring the murder'd body, some the murderers:

Let them not speak a word,—the guilt is plain;

For, by my soul, were there worse end than death,

That end upon them should be executed.

TAMORA.

Andronicus, I will entreat the king:

Fear not thy sons; they shall do well enough.

TITUS.

Come, Lucius, come; stay not to talk with them.

[Exeunt severally. Attendants bearing the body.]

SCENE IV. Another part of the Forest.

[Enter DEMETRIUS and CHIRON, with LAVINIA, ravished; her hands cut off, and her tongue cut out.]

DEMETRIUS.

So, now go tell, an if thy tongue can speak,

Who 'twas that cut thy tongue and ravish'd thee.

CHIRON.

Write down thy mind, bewray thy meaning so,

An if thy stumps will let thee play the scribe.

DEMETRIUS.

See how with signs and tokens she can scrowl.

CHIRON.

Go home, call for sweet water, wash thy hands.

DEMETRIUS.

She hath no tongue to call, nor hands to wash;

And so let's leave her to her silent walks.

CHIRON.

An 'twere my case, I should go hang myself.

DEMETRIUS.

If thou hadst hands to help thee knit the cord.

[Exeunt DEMETRIUS and CHIRON.]

[Enter MARCUS.]

MARCUS.

Who is this?—my niece,—that flies away so fast?

Cousin, a word; where is your husband?—

If I do dream, would all my wealth would wake me!

If I do wake, some planet strike me down,

That I may slumber an eternal sleep!—

Speak, gentle niece,—what stern ungentle hands

Hath lopp'd, and hew'd, and made thy body bare

Of her two branches,—those sweet ornaments

Whose circling shadows kings have sought to sleep in,

And might not gain so great a happiness

As half thy love? Why dost not speak to me?—

Alas, a crimson river of warm blood,

Like to a bubbling fountain stirr'd with wind,

Doth rise and fall between thy rosed lips,

Coming and going with thy honey breath.

But sure some Tereus hath deflowered thee,

And, lest thou shouldst detect him, cut thy tongue.

Ah, now thou turn'st away thy face for shame:

And notwithstanding all this loss of blood,—

As from a conduit with three issuing spouts,—

Yet do thy cheeks look red as Titan's face

Blushing to be encounter'd with a cloud.

Shall I speak for thee? shall I say 'tis so?

O, that I knew thy heart, and knew the beast,

That I might rail at him, to ease my mind!

Sorrow concealed, like an oven stopp'd,

Doth burn the heart to cinders where it is.

Fair Philomela, why she but lost her tongue,

And in a tedious sampler sew'd her mind;

But, lovely niece, that mean is cut from thee;

A craftier Tereus, cousin, hast thou met,

And he hath cut those pretty fingers off

That could have better sew'd than Philomel.

O, had the monster seen those lily hands

Tremble, like aspen leaves, upon a lute,

And make the silken strings delight to kiss them,

He would not then have touch'd them for his life!

Or had he heard the heavenly harmony

Which that sweet tongue hath made,

He would have dropp'd his knife, and fell asleep,

As Cerberus at the Thracian poet's feet.

Come, let us go, and make thy father blind;

For such a sight will blind a father's eye:

One hour's storm will drown the fragrant meads;

What will whole months of tears thy father's eyes?

Do not draw back, for we will mourn with thee:

O, could our mourning case thy misery!

[Exeunt.]

71

ACT III.

SCENE I. Rome. A street.

[Enter Senators, Tribunes, and Officers of Justice, with MARTIUS and QUINTUS bound, passing on to the place of execution; TITUS going before, pleading.]

TITUS.

Hear me, grave fathers! noble tribunes, stay!

For pity of mine age, whose youth was spent

In dangerous wars whilst you securely slept;

For all my blood in Rome's great quarrel shed;

For all the frosty nights that I have watch'd;

And for these bitter tears, which now you see

Filling the aged wrinkles in my cheeks;

Be pitiful to my condemned sons,

Whose souls are not corrupted as 'tis thought.

For two and twenty sons I never wept,

Because they died in honour's lofty bed.

[Throwing himself on the ground.]

For these, tribunes, in the dust I write

My heart's deep languor and my soul's sad tears:

Let my tears stanch the earth's dry appetite;

My sons' sweet blood will make it shame and blush.

[Exeunt Senators, Tribunes, &c., with the prisoners.]

O earth, I will befriend thee more with rain

That shall distil from these two ancient urns,

Than youthful April shall with all his showers:

In summer's drought I'll drop upon thee still;

In winter with warm tears I'll melt the snow,

And keep eternal spring-time on thy face,

So thou refuse to drink my dear sons' blood.

[Enter Lucius with his sword drawn.]

O reverend tribunes! O gentle aged men!

Unbind my sons, reverse the doom of death;

And let me say, that never wept before,

My tears are now prevailing orators.

LUCIUS.

O noble father, you lament in vain:

The tribunes hear you not, no man is by;

And you recount your sorrows to a stone.

TITUS.

Ah, Lucius, for thy brothers let me plead.—

Grave tribunes, once more I entreat of you.

LUCIUS.

My gracious lord, no tribune hears you speak.

TITUS.

Why, 'tis no matter, man: if they did hear,

They would not mark me; if they did mark,

They would not pity me; yet plead I must,

And bootless unto them.

Therefore I tell my sorrows to the stones;

Who, though they cannot answer my distress,

Yet in some sort they are better than the tribunes,

For that they will not intercept my tale:

When I do weep they humbly at my feet

Receive my tears, and seem to weep with me;

And were they but attired in grave weeds,

Rome could afford no tribunes like to these.

A stone is soft as wax, tribunes more hard than stones;

A stone is silent, and offendeth not,—

And tribunes with their tongues doom men to death.

[Rises.]

But wherefore stand'st thou with thy weapon drawn?

LUCIUS.

To rescue my two brothers from their death:

For which attempt the judges have pronounc'd

My everlasting doom of banishment.

TITUS.

O happy man! they have befriended thee.

Why, foolish Lucius, dost thou not perceive

That Rome is but a wilderness of tigers?

Tigers must prey; and Rome affords no prey

But me and mine: how happy art thou, then,

From these devourers to be banished!—

But who comes with our brother Marcus here?

[Enter MARCUS and LAVINIA.]

MARCUS.

Titus, prepare thy aged eyes to weep;

Or if not so, thy noble heart to break:

I bring consuming sorrow to thine age.

TITUS.

Will it consume me? let me see it then.

MARCUS.

This was thy daughter.

TITUS.

Why, Marcus, so she is.

LUCIUS.

Ay me! this object kills me!

TITUS.

Faint-hearted boy, arise, and look upon her.—

Speak, my Lavinia, what accursed hand

Hath made thee handless in thy father's sight?

What fool hath added water to the sea,

Or brought a fagot to bright-burning Troy?

My grief was at the height before thou cam'st;

And now, like Nilus, it disdaineth bounds.

Give me a sword, I'll chop off my hands too;

For they have fought for Rome, and all in vain;

And they have nurs'd this woe in feeding life;

In bootless prayer have they been held up,

And they have serv'd me to effectless use:

Now all the service I require of them

Is that the one will help to cut the other.—

'Tis well, Lavinia, that thou hast no hands;

For hands to do Rome service, are but vain.

LUCIUS.

Speak, gentle sister, who hath martyr'd thee?

MARCUS.

O, that delightful engine of her thoughts,

That blabb'd them with such pleasing eloquence,

Is torn from forth that pretty hollow cage,

Where, like a sweet melodious bird, it sung

Sweet varied notes, enchanting every ear!

LUCIUS.

O, say thou for her, who hath done this deed?

MARCUS.

O, thus I found her straying in the park,

Seeking to hide herself, as doth the deer

That hath receiv'd some unrecuring wound.

TITUS.

It was my deer; and he that wounded her

Hath hurt me more than had he kill'd me dead:

For now I stand as one upon a rock,

Environ'd with a wilderness of sea;

Who marks the waxing tide grow wave by wave,

Expecting ever when some envious surge

Will in his brinish bowels swallow him.

This way to death my wretched sons are gone;

Here stands my other son, a banish'd man;

And here my brother, weeping at my woes:

But that which gives my soul the greatest spurn

Is dear Lavinia, dearer than my soul.—

Had I but seen thy picture in this plight

It would have madded me: what shall I do

Now I behold thy lively body so?

Thou hast no hands to wipe away thy tears,

Nor tongue to tell me who hath martyr'd thee:

Thy husband he is dead; and for his death

Thy brothers are condemn'd, and dead by this.—

Look, Marcus!—ah, son Lucius, look on her!

When I did name her brothers, then fresh tears

Stood on her cheeks, as doth the honey dew

Upon a gather'd lily almost wither'd.

MARCUS.

Perchance she weeps because they kill'd her husband:

Perchance because she knows them innocent.

TITUS.

If they did kill thy husband, then be joyful,

Because the law hath ta'en revenge on them.—

No, no, they would not do so foul a deed;

Witness the sorrow that their sister makes.—

Gentle Lavinia, let me kiss thy lips;

Or make some sign how I may do thee ease:

Shall thy good uncle, and thy brother Lucius,

And thou, and I, sit round about some fountain,

Looking all downwards, to behold our cheeks

How they are stain'd, like meadows yet not dry,

With miry slime left on them by a flood?

And in the fountain shall we gaze so long,

Till the fresh taste be taken from that clearness,

And made a brine-pit with our bitter tears?

Or shall we cut away our hands like thine?

Or shall we bite our tongues, and in dumb shows

Pass the remainder of our hateful days?

What shall we do? let us, that have our tongues,

Plot some device of further misery,

To make us wonder'd at in time to come.

LUCIUS.

Sweet father, cease your tears; for at your grief

See how my wretched sister sobs and weeps.

MARCUS.

Patience, dear niece.—Good Titus, dry thine eyes.

TITUS.

Ah, Marcus, Marcus! brother, well I wot

Thy napkin cannot drink a tear of mine,

For thou, poor man, hast drown'd it with thine own.

LUCIUS.

Ah, my Lavinia, I will wipe thy cheeks.

TITUS.

Mark, Marcus, mark! I understand her signs:

Had she a tongue to speak, now would she say

That to her brother which I said to thee:

His napkin, with his true tears all bewet,

Can do no service on her sorrowful cheeks.

O, what a sympathy of woe is this,—

As far from help as limbo is from bliss!

[Enter AARON.]

AARON.

Titus Andronicus, my lord the emperor

Sends thee this word,—that, if thou love thy sons,

Let Marcus, Lucius, or thyself, old Titus,

Or any one of you, chop off your hand

And send it to the king: he for the same

Will send thee hither both thy sons alive:

And that shall be the ransom for their fault.

TITUS.

O gracious emperor! O gentle Aaron!

Did ever raven sing so like a lark

That gives sweet tidings of the sun's uprise?

With all my heart I'll send the emperor

My hand:

Good Aaron, wilt thou help to chop it off?

LUCIUS.

Stay, father! for that noble hand of thine,

That hath thrown down so many enemies,

Shall not be sent: my hand will serve the turn:

My youth can better spare my blood than you;

And therefore mine shall save my brothers' lives.

MARCUS.

Which of your hands hath not defended Rome,

And rear'd aloft the bloody battle-axe,

Writing destruction on the enemy's castle?

O, none of both but are of high desert:

My hand hath been but idle; let it serve

To ransom my two nephews from their death;

Then have I kept it to a worthy end.

AARON.

Nay, come, agree whose hand shall go along,

For fear they die before their pardon come.

MARCUS.

My hand shall go.

LUCIUS.

By heaven, it shall not go!

TITUS.

Sirs, strive no more: such wither'd herbs as these

Are meet for plucking up, and therefore mine.

LUCIUS.

Sweet father, if I shall be thought thy son,

Let me redeem my brothers both from death.

MARCUS.

And for our father's sake and mother's care,

Now let me show a brother's love to thee.

TITUS.

Agree between you; I will spare my hand.

LUCIUS.

Then I'll go fetch an axe.

MARCUS.

But I will use the axe.

[Exeunt LUCIUS and MARCUS.]

TITUS.

Come hither, Aaron; I'll deceive them both:

Lend me thy hand, and I will give thee mine.

AARON.

[Aside.] If that be call'd deceit, I will be honest,

And never whilst I live deceive men so:—

But I'll deceive you in another sort,

And that you'll say ere half an hour pass.

[He cuts off TITUS'S hand.]

[Re-enter LUCIUS and MARCUS.]

TITUS.

Now stay your strife: what shall be is despatch'd.—

Good Aaron, give his majesty my hand:

Tell him it was a hand that warded him

From thousand dangers; bid him bury it;

More hath it merited,—that let it have.

As for my sons, say I account of them

As jewels purchas'd at an easy price;

And yet dear too, because I bought mine own.

AARON.

I go, Andronicus: and for thy hand

Look by and by to have thy sons with thee:—

[Aside] Their heads I mean. O, how this villainy

Doth fat me with the very thoughts of it!

Let fools do good, and fair men call for grace:

Aaron will have his soul black like his face.

[Exit.]

TITUS.

O, here I lift this one hand up to heaven,

And bow this feeble ruin to the earth:

If any power pities wretched tears,

To that I call!—[To LAVINIA.] What, wilt thou kneel with me?

Do, then, dear heart; for heaven shall hear our prayers;

Or with our sighs we'll breathe the welkin dim,

And stain the sun with fog, as sometime clouds

When they do hug him in their melting bosoms.

MARCUS.

O brother, speak with possibilities,

And do not break into these deep extremes.

TITUS.

Is not my sorrow deep, having no bottom?

Then be my passions bottomless with them.

MARCUS.

But yet let reason govern thy lament.

TITUS.

If there were reason for these miseries,

Then into limits could I bind my woes:

When heaven doth weep, doth not the earth o'erflow?

If the winds rage, doth not the sea wax mad,

Threatening the welkin with his big-swol'n face?

And wilt thou have a reason for this coil?

I am the sea; hark, how her sighs do flow!

She is the weeping welkin, I the earth:

Then must my sea be moved with her sighs;

Then must my earth with her continual tears

Become a deluge, overflow'd and drown'd;

For why my bowels cannot hide her woes,

But like a drunkard must I vomit them.

Then give me leave; for losers will have leave

To ease their stomachs with their bitter tongues.

[**Enter a Messenger, with two heads and a hand.**]

MESSENGER.

Worthy Andronicus, ill art thou repaid

For that good hand thou sent'st the emperor.

Here are the heads of thy two noble sons;

And here's thy hand, in scorn to thee sent back,—

Thy grief their sports, thy resolution mock'd:

That woe is me to think upon thy woes,

More than remembrance of my father's death.

[Exit.]

MARCUS.

Now let hot Aetna cool in Sicily,

And be my heart an ever-burning hell!

These miseries are more than may be borne.

To weep with them that weep doth ease some deal;

But sorrow flouted at is double death.

LUCIUS.

Ah, that this sight should make so deep a wound,

And yet detested life not shrink thereat!

That ever death should let life bear his name,

Where life hath no more interest but to breathe!

[LAVINIA kisses him.]

MARCUS.

Alas, poor heart, that kiss is comfortless

As frozen water to a starved snake.

TITUS.

When will this fearful slumber have an end?

MARCUS.

Now farewell, flattery; die, Andronicus;

Thou dost not slumber: see thy two sons' heads,

Thy warlike hand, thy mangled daughter here;

Thy other banish'd son with this dear sight

Struck pale and bloodless; and thy brother, I,

Even like a stony image, cold and numb.

Ah! now no more will I control thy griefs:

Rent off thy silver hair, thy other hand

Gnawing with thy teeth; and be this dismal sight

The closing up of our most wretched eyes:

Now is a time to storm; why art thou still?

TITUS.

Ha, ha, ha!

MARCUS.

Why dost thou laugh? it fits not with this hour.

TITUS.

Why, I have not another tear to shed:

Besides, this sorrow is an enemy,

And would usurp upon my watery eyes,

And make them blind with tributary tears:

Then which way shall I find revenge's cave?

For these two heads do seem to speak to me,

And threat me I shall never come to bliss

Till all these mischiefs be return'd again

Even in their throats that have committed them.

Come, let me see what task I have to do.—

You heavy people circle me about,

That I may turn me to each one of you,

And swear unto my soul to right your wrongs.—

The vow is made.—Come, brother, take a head;

And in this hand the other will I bear.

And, Lavinia, thou shalt be employ'd in these things;

Bear thou my hand, sweet wench, between thy teeth.

As for thee, boy, go, get thee from my sight;

Thou art an exile, and thou must not stay:

Hie to the Goths, and raise an army there:

And if you love me, as I think you do,

Let's kiss and part, for we have much to do.

[Exeunt TITUS, MARCUS, and LAVINIA.]

LUCIUS.

Farewell, Andronicus, my noble father,—

The woefull'st man that ever liv'd in Rome:

Farewell, proud Rome; till Lucius come again,

He leaves his pledges dearer than his life:

Farewell, Lavinia, my noble sister;

O, would thou wert as thou 'tofore hast been!

But now nor Lucius nor Lavinia lives

But in oblivion and hateful griefs.

If Lucius live, he will requite your wrongs,

And make proud Saturnine and his empress

Beg at the gates, like Tarquin and his queen.

Now will I to the Goths, and raise a power

To be reveng'd on Rome and Saturnine.

[Exit.]

SCENE II. Rome. A Room in TITUS'S House. A banquet set out.

[Enter TITUS, MARCUS, LAVINIA, and YOUNG LUCIUS, a boy.]

TITUS.

So so, now sit: and look you eat no more

Than will preserve just so much strength in us

As will revenge these bitter woes of ours.

Marcus, unknit that sorrow-wreathen knot:

Thy niece and I, poor creatures, want our hands,

And cannot passionate our tenfold grief

With folded arms. This poor right hand of mine

Is left to tyrannize upon my breast;

And, when my heart, all mad with misery,

Beats in this hollow prison of my flesh,

Then thus I thump it down.—

[To LAVINIA] Thou map of woe, that thus dost talk in signs!

When thy poor heart beats with outrageous beating,

Thou canst not strike it thus to make it still.

Wound it with sighing, girl; kill it with groans;

Or get some little knife between thy teeth,

And just against thy heart make thou a hole,

That all the tears that thy poor eyes let fall

May run into that sink, and, soaking in,

Drown the lamenting fool in sea-salt tears.

MARCUS.

Fie, brother, fie! teach her not thus to lay

Such violent hands upon her tender life.

TITUS.

How now! has sorrow made thee dote already?

Why, Marcus, no man should be mad but I.

What violent hands can she lay on her life?

Ah, wherefore dost thou urge the name of hands;—

To bid Aeneas tell the tale twice o'er

How Troy was burnt and he made miserable?

O, handle not the theme, to talk of hands,

Lest we remember still that we have none.—

Fie, fie, how frantically I square my talk,—

As if we should forget we had no hands,

If Marcus did not name the word of hands!—

Come, let's fall to; and, gentle girl, eat this.—

Here is no drink! Hark, Marcus, what she says;—

I can interpret all her martyr'd signs;—

She says she drinks no other drink but tears,

Brew'd with her sorrow, mesh'd upon her cheeks:—

Speechless complainer, I will learn thy thought;

In thy dumb action will I be as perfect

As begging hermits in their holy prayers:

Thou shalt not sigh, nor hold thy stumps to heaven,

Nor wink, nor nod, nor kneel, nor make a sign,

But I of these will wrest an alphabet,

And by still practice learn to know thy meaning.

BOY.

Good grandsire, leave these bitter deep laments:

Make my aunt merry with some pleasing tale.

MARCUS.

Alas, the tender boy, in passion mov'd,

Doth weep to see his grandsire's heaviness.

TITUS.

Peace, tender sapling; thou art made of tears,

And tears will quickly melt thy life away.—

                      [MARCUS strikes the dish with a knife.]

What dost thou strike at, Marcus, with thy knife?

MARCUS.

At that that I have kill'd, my lord,—a fly.

TITUS.

Out on thee, murderer! thou kill'st my heart;

Mine eyes are cloy'd with view of tyranny:

A deed of death done on the innocent

Becomes not Titus' brother: get thee gone;

I see thou art not for my company.

MARCUS.

Alas, my lord, I have but kill'd a fly.

TITUS.

But how if that fly had a father and mother?

How would he hang his slender gilded wings

And buzz lamenting doings in the air!

Poor harmless fly,

That with his pretty buzzing melody

Came here to make us merry! and thou hast kill'd him.

MARCUS.

Pardon me, sir; 'twas a black ill-favour'd fly,

Like to the empress' Moor; therefore I kill'd him.

TITUS.

O, O, O!

Then pardon me for reprehending thee,

For thou hast done a charitable deed.

Give me thy knife, I will insult on him,

Flattering myself as if it were the Moor

Come hither purposely to poison me.—

There's for thyself, and that's for Tamora.—

Ah, sirrah!

Yet, I think, we are not brought so low

But that between us we can kill a fly

That comes in likeness of a coal-black Moor.

MARCUS.

Alas, poor man! grief has so wrought on him,

He takes false shadows for true substances.

TITUS.

Come, take away.—Lavinia, go with me;

I'll to thy closet; and go read with thee

Sad stories chanced in the times of old.—

Come, boy, and go with me: thy sight is young,

And thou shalt read when mine begin to dazzle.

[Exeunt.]

ACT IV.

SCENE I. Rome. Before TITUS'S House.

[Enter TITUS and MARCUS. Then enter YOUNG LUCIUS running, with books under his arm, and LAVINIA running after him.]

YOUNG LUCIUS.

Help, grandsire, help! my aunt Lavinia

Follows me everywhere, I know not why.—

Good uncle Marcus, see how swift she comes!

Alas, sweet aunt, I know not what you mean.

MARCUS.

Stand by me, Lucius: do not fear thine aunt.

TITUS.

She loves thee, boy, too well to do thee harm.

YOUNG LUCIUS

Ay, when my father was in Rome she did.

MARCUS.

What means my niece Lavinia by these signs?

TITUS.

Fear her not, Lucius: somewhat doth she mean:—

See, Lucius, see how much she makes of thee:

Somewhither would she have thee go with her.

Ah, boy, Cornelia never with more care

Read to her sons than she hath read to thee

Sweet poetry and Tully's Orator.

MARCUS.

Canst thou not guess wherefore she plies thee thus?

YOUNG LUCIUS.

My lord, I know not, I, nor can I guess,

Unless some fit or frenzy do possess her:

For I have heard my grandsire say full oft

Extremity of griefs would make men mad;

And I have read that Hecuba of Troy

Ran mad for sorrow: that made me to fear;

Although, my lord, I know my noble aunt

Loves me as dear as e'er my mother did,

And would not, but in fury, fright my youth:

Which made me down to throw my books, and fly,—

Causeless, perhaps: but pardon me, sweet aunt:

And, madam, if my uncle Marcus go,

I will most willingly attend your ladyship.

MARCUS.

Lucius, I will.

[LAVINIA turns over with her stumps the books which Lucius has let
fall.]

TITUS.

How now, Lavinia!—Marcus, what means this?

Some book there is that she desires to see.

Which is it, girl, of these?—Open them, boy.—

But thou art deeper read and better skill'd:

Come and take choice of all my library,

And so beguile thy sorrow, till the heavens

Reveal the damn'd contriver of this deed.—

Why lifts she up her arms in sequence thus?

MARCUS.

I think she means that there were more than one

Confederate in the fact;—ay, more there was,

Or else to heaven she heaves them for revenge.

TITUS.

Lucius, what book is that she tosseth so?

YOUNG LUCIUS.

Grandsire, 'tis Ovid's Metamorphosis;

My mother gave it me.

MARCUS.

For love of her that's gone,

Perhaps she cull'd it from among the rest.

TITUS.

Soft! So busily she turns the leaves! Help her:

What would she find?—Lavinia, shall I read?

William Shakespeare

This is the tragic tale of Philomel,

And treats of Tereus' treason and his rape;

And rape, I fear, was root of thy annoy.

MARCUS.

See, brother, see; note how she quotes the leaves.

TITUS.

Lavinia, wert thou thus surpris'd, sweet girl,

Ravish'd, and wrong'd, as Philomela was,

Forc'd in the ruthless, vast, and gloomy woods?—

See, see!—

Ay, such a place there is where we did hunt.—

O, had we never, never hunted there!—

Pattern'd by that the poet here describes,

By nature made for murders and for rapes.

MARCUS.

O, why should nature build so foul a den,

Unless the gods delight in tragedies?

TITUS.

Give signs, sweet girl,—for here are none but friends,—

What Roman lord it was durst do the deed:

Or slunk not Saturnine, as Tarquin erst,

That left the camp to sin in Lucrece' bed?

MARCUS.

97

Sit down, sweet niece:—brother, sit down by me.—

Apollo, Pallas, Jove, or Mercury,

Inspire me, that I may this treason find!—

My lord, look here:—look here, Lavinia:

This sandy plot is plain; guide, if thou canst,

This after me, when I have writ my name

Without the help of any hand at all.

[He writes his name with his staff, guiding it with feet and mouth.]

Curs'd be that heart that forc'd us to this shift!—

Write thou, good niece; and here display at last

What God will have discover'd for revenge:

Heaven guide thy pen to print thy sorrows plain,

That we may know the traitors and the truth!

[She takes the staff in her mouth, guides it with her stumps, and writes.]

TITUS.

O, do ye read, my lord, what she hath writ?

'Stuprum—Chiron—Demetrius.'

MARCUS.

What, what!—the lustful sons of Tamora

Performers of this heinous bloody deed?

TITUS.

Magni Dominator poli,

Tam lentus audis scelera? tam lentus vides?

MARCUS.

O, calm thee, gentle lord; although I know

There is enough written upon this earth

To stir a mutiny in the mildest thoughts,

And arm the minds of infants to exclaims,

My lord, kneel down with me; Lavinia, kneel;

And kneel, sweet boy, the Roman Hector's hope;

And swear with me,—as, with the woeful fere

And father of that chaste dishonour'd dame,

Lord Junius Brutus sware for Lucrece' rape,—

That we will prosecute, by good advice,

Mortal revenge upon these traitorous Goths,

And see their blood, or die with this reproach.

TITUS.

'Tis sure enough, an you knew how.

But if you hunt these bear-whelps, then beware:

The dam will wake; and if she wind you once,

She's with the lion deeply still in league,

And lulls him whilst she playeth on her back,

And when he sleeps will she do what she list.

You are a young huntsman, Marcus; let alone;

And, come, I will go get a leaf of brass,

And with a gad of steel will write these words,

And lay it by: the angry northern wind

Will blow these sands like Sibyl's leaves, abroad,

And where's our lesson, then?—Boy, what say you?

YOUNG LUCIUS.

I say, my lord, that if I were a man,

Their mother's bedchamber should not be safe

For these bad-bondmen to the yoke of Rome.

MARCUS.

Ay, that's my boy! thy father hath full oft

For his ungrateful country done the like.

YOUNG LUCIUS.

And, uncle, so will I, an if I live.

TITUS.

Come, go with me into mine armoury;

Lucius, I'll fit thee; and withal, my boy,

Shall carry from me to the empress' sons

Presents that I intend to send them both:

Come, come; thou'lt do my message, wilt thou not?

YOUNG LUCIUS.

Ay, with my dagger in their bosoms, grandsire.

TITUS.

No, boy, not so; I'll teach thee another course.—

Lavinia, come.—Marcus, look to my house:

Lucius and I'll go brave it at the court;

Ay, marry, will we, sir: and we'll be waited on.

[Exeunt TITUS, LAVINIA, and YOUNG LUCIUS.]

MARCUS.

O heavens, can you hear a good man groan,

And not relent, or not compassion him?

Marcus, attend him in his ecstasy,

That hath more scars of sorrow in his heart

Than foemen's marks upon his batter'd shield;

But yet so just that he will not revenge:—

Revenge, ye heavens, for old Andronicus!

[Exit.]

SCENE II. Rome. A Room in the Palace.

[Enter AARON, DEMETRIUS and CHIRON, at one door; at another
door, YOUNG LUCIUS and an Attendant, with a bundle of weapons,
and verses writ upon them.]

CHIRON.

Demetrius, here's the son of Lucius;

He hath some message to deliver us.

AARON.

Ay, some mad message from his mad grandfather.

YOUNG LUCIUS.

My lords, with all the humbleness I may,

I greet your honours from Andronicus,—

[Aside.] And pray the Roman gods confound you both!

DEMETRIUS.

Gramercy, lovely Lucius: what's the news?

YOUNG LUCIUS.

[Aside] That you are both decipher'd, that's the news,

For villains mark'd with rape.—May it please you,

My grandsire, well advis'd, hath sent by me

The goodliest weapons of his armoury

To gratify your honourable youth,

The hope of Rome; for so he bid me say;

And so I do, and with his gifts present

Your lordships, that, whenever you have need,

You may be armed and appointed well:

And so I leave you both—[aside] like bloody villains.

[Exeunt YOUNG LUCIUS and Attendant.]

DEMETRIUS.

What's here? A scroll; and written round about?

Let's see:

[Reads.] 'Integer vitae, scelerisque purus,

Non eget Mauri jaculis, nec arcu.'

CHIRON.

O, 'tis a verse in Horace, I know it well:

I read it in the grammar long ago.

AARON.

Ay, just,—a verse in Horace;—right, you have it.—

[Aside] Now, what a thing it is to be an ass!

Here's no sound jest! the old man hath found their guilt;

And sends them weapons wrapp'd about with lines,

That wound, beyond their feeling, to the quick.

But were our witty empress well afoot,

She would applaud Andronicus' conceit.

But let her rest in her unrest awhile.—

And now, young lords, was't not a happy star

Led us to Rome, strangers, and more than so,

Captives, to be advanced to this height?

It did me good before the palace gate

To brave the tribune in his brother's hearing.

DEMETRIUS.

But me more good to see so great a lord

Basely insinuate and send us gifts.

AARON.

Had he not reason, Lord Demetrius?

Did you not use his daughter very friendly?

DEMETRIUS.

I would we had a thousand Roman dames

At such a bay, by turn to serve our lust.

CHIRON.

A charitable wish, and full of love.

AARON.

Here lacks but your mother for to say amen.

CHIRON.

And that would she for twenty thousand more.

DEMETRIUS.

Come, let us go; and pray to all the gods

For our beloved mother in her pains.

AARON.

[Aside.] Pray to the devils; the gods have given us over.

[Flourish within.]

DEMETRIUS.

Why do the emperor's trumpets flourish thus?

CHIRON.

Belike, for joy the emperor hath a son.

DEMETRIUS.

Soft! who comes here?

[Enter a NURSE, with a blackamoor CHILD in her arms.]

NURSE.

Good morrow, lords:

O, tell me, did you see Aaron the Moor?

AARON.

Well, more or less, or ne'er a whit at all,

Here Aaron is; and what with Aaron now?

NURSE.

O gentle Aaron, we are all undone!

Now help, or woe betide thee evermore!

AARON.

Why, what a caterwauling dost thou keep!

What dost thou wrap and fumble in thy arms?

NURSE.

O, that which I would hide from heaven's eye,

Our empress' shame and stately Rome's disgrace!—

She is deliver'd, lords,—she is deliver'd.

AARON.

To whom?

NURSE.

I mean, she's brought a-bed.

AARON.

Well, God give her good rest! What hath he sent her?

NURSE.

A devil.

AARON.

Why, then she is the devil's dam; a joyful issue.

NURSE.

A joyless, dismal, black, and sorrowful issue:

Here is the babe, as loathsome as a toad

Amongst the fairest breeders of our clime:

The empress sends it thee, thy stamp, thy seal,

And bids thee christen it with thy dagger's point.

AARON.

Zounds, ye whore! is black so base a hue?—

Sweet blowse, you are a beauteous blossom sure.

DEMETRIUS.

Villain, what hast thou done?

AARON.

That which thou canst not undo.

CHIRON.

Thou hast undone our mother.

AARON.

Villain, I have done thy mother.

DEMETRIUS.

And therein, hellish dog, thou hast undone.

Woe to her chance, and damn'd her loathed choice!

Accurs'd the offspring of so foul a fiend!

CHIRON.

It shall not live.

AARON.

It shall not die.

NURSE.

Aaron, it must; the mother wills it so.

AARON.

What, must it, nurse? then let no man but I

Do execution on my flesh and blood.

DEMETRIUS.

I'll broach the tadpole on my rapier's point:—

Nurse, give it me; my sword shall soon despatch it.

AARON.

Sooner this sword shall plough thy bowels up.

[Takes the CHILD from the NURSE, and draws.]

Stay, murderous villains, will you kill your brother?

Now, by the burning tapers of the sky,

That shone so brightly when this boy was got,

107

He dies upon my scimitar's sharp point

That touches this my first-born son and heir!

I tell you, younglings, not Enceladus,

With all his threatening band of Typhon's brood,

Nor great Alcides, nor the god of war,

Shall seize this prey out of his father's hands.

What, what, ye sanguine, shallow-hearted boys!

Ye white-lim'd walls! ye alehouse-painted signs!

Coal-black is better than another hue,

In that it scorns to bear another hue;

For all the water in the ocean

Can never turn the swan's black legs to white,

Although she lave them hourly in the flood.

Tell the empress from me I am of age

To keep mine own,—excuse it how she can.

DEMETRIUS.

Wilt thou betray thy noble mistress thus?

AARON.

My mistress is my mistress: this my self,—

The vigour and the picture of my youth:

This before all the world do I prefer;

This maugre all the world will I keep safe,

Or some of you shall smoke for it in Rome.

DEMETRIUS.

By this our mother is for ever sham'd.

CHIRON.

Rome will despise her for this foul escape.

NURSE.

The emperor, in his rage, will doom her death.

CHIRON.

I blush to think upon this ignomy.

AARON.

Why, there's the privilege your beauty bears:

Fie, treacherous hue, that will betray with blushing

The close enacts and counsels of thy heart!

Here's a young lad fram'd of another leer:

Look how the black slave smiles upon the father,

As who should say 'Old lad, I am thine own.'

He is your brother, lords; sensibly fed

Of that self-blood that first gave life to you;

And from your womb where you imprison'd were

He is enfranchised and come to light:

Nay, he is your brother by the surer side,

Although my seal be stamped in his face.

NURSE.

Aaron, what shall I say unto the empress?

DEMETRIUS.

Advise thee, Aaron, what is to be done,

And we will all subscribe to thy advice:

Save thou the child, so we may all be safe.

AARON.

Then sit we down and let us all consult.

My son and I will have the wind of you:

Keep there: now talk at pleasure of your safety.

[They sit.]

DEMETRIUS.

How many women saw this child of his?

AARON.

Why, so, brave lords! when we join in league

I am a lamb: but if you brave the Moor,

The chafed boar, the mountain lioness,

The ocean swells not so as Aaron storms.—

But say, again, how many saw the child?

NURSE.

Cornelia the midwife and myself;

And no one else but the deliver'd empress.

AARON.

The empress, the midwife, and yourself:

Two may keep counsel when the third's away:

Go to the empress, tell her this I said:—

[Stabs her, and she dies.]

Weke, weke!—so cries a pig prepar'd to the spit.

DEMETRIUS.

What mean'st thou, Aaron? Wherefore didst thou this?

AARON.

O Lord, sir, 'tis a deed of policy:

Shall she live to betray this guilt of ours,—

A long-tongu'd babbling gossip? no, lords, no:

And now be it known to you my full intent.

Not far, one Muliteus lives, my countryman;

His wife but yesternight was brought to bed;

His child is like to her, fair as you are:

Go pack with him, and give the mother gold,

And tell them both the circumstance of all;

And how by this their child shall be advanc'd,

And be received for the emperor's heir,

And substituted in the place of mine,

To calm this tempest whirling in the court;

And let the emperor dandle him for his own.

Hark ye, lords; ye see I have given her physic.

[Pointing to the NURSE.]

And you must needs bestow her funeral;

The fields are near, and you are gallant grooms:

This done, see that you take no longer days,

But send the midwife presently to me.

The midwife and the nurse well made away,

Then let the ladies tattle what they please.

CHIRON.

Aaron, I see thou wilt not trust the air

With secrets.

DEMETRIUS.

For this care of Tamora,

Herself and hers are highly bound to thee.

[Exeunt DEMETRIUS and CHIRON, bearing off the dead NURSE.]

AARON.

Now to the Goths, as swift as swallow flies;

There to dispose this treasure in mine arms,

And secretly to greet the empress' friends.—

Come on, you thick-lipp'd slave, I'll bear you hence;

For it is you that puts us to our shifts:

I'll make you feed on berries and on roots,

And feed on curds and whey, and suck the goat,

And cabin in a cave, and bring you up

To be a warrior and command a camp.

[Exit.]

SCENE III. Rome. A public Place.

[Enter TITUS, bearing arrows with letters at the ends of them; with him MARCUS, YOUNG LUCIUS, and other gentlemen, with bows.]

TITUS.

Come, Marcus, come:—kinsmen, this is the way.—

Sir boy, let me see your archery;

Look ye draw home enough, and 'tis there straight.—

Terras Astrea reliquit:

Be you remember'd, Marcus; she's gone, she's fled.

Sirs, take you to your tools. You, cousins, shall

Go sound the ocean and cast your nets;

Happily you may catch her in the sea;

Yet there's as little justice as at land.—

No; Publius and Sempronius, you must do it;

'Tis you must dig with mattock and with spade,

And pierce the inmost centre of the earth:

Then, when you come to Pluto's region,

I pray you deliver him this petition;

Tell him it is for justice and for aid,

And that it comes from old Andronicus,

Shaken with sorrows in ungrateful Rome.—

Ah, Rome!—Well, well; I made thee miserable

What time I threw the people's suffrages

On him that thus doth tyrannize o'er me.—

Go, get you gone; and pray be careful all,

And leave you not a man-of-war unsearch'd:

This wicked emperor may have shipp'd her hence;

And, kinsmen, then we may go pipe for justice.

MARCUS.

O Publius, is not this a heavy case,

To see thy noble uncle thus distract?

PUBLIUS.

Therefore, my lords, it highly us concerns

By day and night to attend him carefully,

And feed his humour kindly as we may,

Till time beget some careful remedy.

MARCUS.

Kinsmen, his sorrows are past remedy.

Join with the Goths; and with revengeful war

Take wreak on Rome for this ingratitude,

And vengeance on the traitor Saturnine.

TITUS.

Publius, how now! how now, my masters!

What, have you met with her?

PUBLIUS.

No, my good lord; but Pluto sends you word,

If you will have Revenge from hell, you shall:

Marry, for Justice, she is so employ'd,

He thinks, with Jove in heaven, or somewhere else,

So that perforce you must needs stay a time.

TITUS.

He doth me wrong to feed me with delays.

I'll dive into the burning lake below,

And pull her out of Acheron by the heels.—

Marcus, we are but shrubs, no cedars we,

No big-bon'd men, fram'd of the Cyclops' size;

But metal, Marcus, steel to the very back,

Yet wrung with wrongs more than our backs can bear:

And, sith there's no justice in earth nor hell,

We will solicit heaven, and move the gods

To send down Justice for to wreak our wrongs.—

Come, to this gear.—You are a good archer, Marcus.

[He gives them the arrows.]

'Ad Jovem' that's for you; here, 'Ad Apollinem':—

'Ad Martem' that's for myself:—

Here, boy, to Pallas:—here, tTo Mercury:—

To Saturn, Caius, not to Saturnine;

You were as good to shoot against the wind.—

To it, boy.—Marcus, loose when I bid.—

115

Of my word, I have written to effect;

There's not a god left unsolicited.

MARCUS.

Kinsmen, shoot all your shafts into the court:

We will afflict the emperor in his pride.

TITUS.

Now, masters, draw. [They shoot.] O, well said, Lucius!

Good boy, in Virgo's lap; give it Pallas.

MARCUS.

My lord, I aim a mile beyond the moon:

Your letter is with Jupiter by this.

TITUS.

Ha! ha!

Publius, Publius, hast thou done?

See, see, thou hast shot off one of Taurus' horns.

MARCUS.

This was the sport, my lord: when Publius shot,

The Bull, being gall'd, gave Aries such a knock

That down fell both the Ram's horns in the court;

And who should find them but the empress' villain?

She laugh'd, and told the Moor he should not choose

But give them to his master for a present.

TITUS.

Why, there it goes: God give his lordship joy!

[Enter a CLOWN, with a basket and two pigeons in it.]

News, news from heaven! Marcus, the post is come.

Sirrah, what tidings? have you any letters?

Shall I have justice? what says Jupiter?

CLOWN. Ho, the gibbet-maker? he says that he hath taken them down again, for the man must not be hanged till the next week.

TITUS.

But what says Jupiter, I ask thee?

CLOWN. Alas, sir, I know not Jupiter; I never drank with him in all my life.

TITUS.

Why, villain, art not thou the carrier?

CLOWN.

Ay, of my pigeons, sir; nothing else.

TITUS.

Why, didst thou not come from heaven?

CLOWN. From heaven! alas, sir, I never came there: God forbid I should be so bold to press to heaven in my young days. Why, I am going with my pigeons to the tribunal plebs, to take up a matter of brawl betwixt my uncle and one of the imperial's men.

MARCUS. Why, sir, that is as fit as can be to serve for your oration; and let him deliver the pigeons to the emperor from you.

TITUS.

Tell me, can you deliver an oration to the emperor with a grace?

CLOWN.

Nay, truly, sir, I could never say grace in all my life.

TITUS.

Sirrah, come hither: make no more ado,

But give your pigeons to the emperor:

By me thou shalt have justice at his hands.

Hold, hold; meanwhile here's money for thy charges.—

Give me pen and ink.—

Sirrah, can you with a grace deliver up a supplication?

CLOWN.

Ay, sir.

TITUS. Then here is a supplication for you. And when you come to him, at the first approach you must kneel; then kiss his foot; then deliver up your pigeons; and then look for your reward. I'll be at hand, sir; see you do it bravely.

CLOWN.

I warrant you, sir; let me alone.

TITUS.

Sirrah, hast thou a knife? Come let me see it.

Here, Marcus, fold it in the oration;

For thou hast made it like a humble suppliant.:—

And when thou hast given it to the emperor,

Knock at my door, and tell me what he says.

CLOWN.

God be with you, sir; I will.

TITUS.

Come, Marcus, let us go.—Publius, follow me.

[Exeunt.]

SCENE IV. Rome. Before the Palace.

[Enter SATURNINUS, TAMORA, DEMETRIUS, CHIRON; Lords, and others; SATURNINUS with the arrows in his hand that TITUS shot.]

SATURNINUS.

Why, lords, what wrongs are these! was ever seen

An emperor in Rome thus overborne,

Troubled, confronted thus; and, for the extent

Of legal justice, us'd in such contempt?

My lords, you know, as know the mightful gods,

However these disturbers of our peace

Buzz in the people's ears, there naught hath pass'd

But even with law, against the wilful sons

Of old Andronicus. And what an if

His sorrows have so overwhelm'd his wits,

Shall we be thus afflicted in his freaks,

His fits, his frenzy, and his bitterness?

And now he writes to heaven for his redress:

See, here's to Jove, and this to Mercury;

This to Apollo; this to the God of War;—

Sweet scrolls to fly about the streets of Rome!

What's this but libelling against the senate,

And blazoning our injustice everywhere?

A goodly humour, is it not, my lords?

As who would say, in Rome no justice were.

But if I live, his feigned ecstasies

Shall be no shelter to these outrages:

But he and his shall know that justice lives

In Saturninus' health; whom, if she sleep,

He'll so awake as he in fury shall

Cut off the proud'st conspirator that lives.

TAMORA.

My gracious lord, my lovely Saturnine,

Lord of my life, commander of my thoughts,

Calm thee, and bear the faults of Titus' age,

The effects of sorrow for his valiant sons,

Whose loss hath pierc'd him deep, and scarr'd his heart;

And rather comfort his distressed plight

Than prosecute the meanest or the best

For these contempts.—[Aside] Why, thus it shall become

High-witted Tamora to gloze with all:

But, Titus, I have touch'd thee to the quick,

Thy life-blood on't; if Aaron now be wise,

Then is all safe, the anchor in the port.—

[Enter CLOWN.]

How now, good fellow! wouldst thou speak with us?

CLOWN.

Yes, forsooth, an your mistership be imperial.

TAMORA.

Empress I am, but yonder sits the emperor.

CLOWN. 'Tis he.—God and Saint Stephen give you good-den; I have brought you a letter and a couple of pigeons here.

[SATURNINUS reads the letter.]

SATURNINUS.

Go take him away, and hang him presently.

CLOWN.

How much money must I have?

TAMORA.

Come, sirrah, you must be hang'd.

CLOWN.

Hang'd! by'r lady, then I have brought up a neck to a fair end.

[Exit guarded.]

SATURNINUS.

Despiteful and intolerable wrongs!

Shall I endure this monstrous villainy?

I know from whence this same device proceeds:

May this be borne,—as if his traitorous sons,

That died by law for murder of our brother,

Have by my means been butchered wrongfully?—

Go, drag the villain hither by the hair;

Nor age nor honour shall shape privilege.—

For this proud mock I'll be thy slaughter-man;

Sly frantic wretch, that holp'st to make me great,

In hope thyself should govern Rome and me.

[**Enter AEMILIUS.**]

What news with thee, Aemilius?

AEMILIUS.

Arm, my lord! Rome never had more cause!

The Goths have gather'd head; and with a power

Of high resolved men, bent to the spoil,

They hither march amain, under conduct

Of Lucius, son to old Andronicus;

Who threats, in course of this revenge, to do

As much as ever Coriolanus did.

SATURNINUS.

Is warlike Lucius general of the Goths?

These tidings nip me; and I hang the head

As flowers with frost, or grass beat down with storms:

Ay, now begins our sorrows to approach:

'Tis he the common people love so much;

Myself hath often overheard them say,—

When I have walked like a private man,—

That Lucius' banishment was wrongfully,

And they have wish'd that Lucius were their emperor.

TAMORA.

Why should you fear? is not your city strong?

SATURNINUS.

Ay, but the citizens favour Lucius,

And will revolt from me to succour him.

TAMORA.

King, be thy thoughts imperious like thy name.

Is the sun dimm'd, that gnats do fly in it?

The eagle suffers little birds to sing,

And is not careful what they mean thereby,

Knowing that with the shadow of his wing

He can at pleasure stint their melody;

Even so mayest thou the giddy men of Rome.

Then cheer thy spirit: for know, thou emperor,

I will enchant the old Andronicus

With words more sweet, and yet more dangerous,

Than baits to fish or honey-stalks to sheep,

Whenas the one is wounded with the bait,

The other rotted with delicious feed.

SATURNINUS.

But he will not entreat his son for us.

TAMORA.

If Tamora entreat him, then he will:

For I can smooth and fill his aged ear

124

With golden promises that, were his heart

Almost impregnable, his old ears deaf,

Yet should both ear and heart obey my tongue.—

Go thou before [to AEMILIUS]; be our ambassador:

Say that the emperor requests a parley

Of warlike Lucius, and appoint the meeting

Even at his father's house, the old Andronicus.

SATURNINUS.

Aemilius, do this message honourably:

And if he stand on hostage for his safety,

Bid him demand what pledge will please him best.

AEMILIUS.

Your bidding shall I do effectually.

[Exit.]

TAMORA.

Now will I to that old Andronicus,

And temper him with all the art I have,

To pluck proud Lucius from the warlike Goths.

And now, sweet emperor, be blithe again,

And bury all thy fear in my devices.

SATURNINUS.

Then go successantly, and plead to him.

[Exeunt.]

ACT V.

SCENE I. Plains near Rome.

[Enter LUCIUS with GOTHS, with drum and colours.]

LUCIUS.

Approved warriors and my faithful friends,

I have received letters from great Rome,

Which signifies what hate they bear their emperor,

And how desirous of our sight they are.

Therefore, great lords, be, as your titles witness,

Imperious and impatient of your wrongs;

And wherein Rome hath done you any scath

Let him make treble satisfaction.

FIRST GOTH.

Brave slip, sprung from the great Andronicus,

Whose name was once our terror, now our comfort;

Whose high exploits and honourable deeds

Ingrateful Rome requites with foul contempt,

Be bold in us: we'll follow where thou lead'st,—

Like stinging bees in hottest summer's day,

Led by their master to the flowered fields,—

And be aveng'd on cursed Tamora.

GOTHS.

And as he saith, so say we all with him.

LUCIUS.

I humbly thank him, and I thank you all.

But who comes here, led by a lusty Goth?

[Enter a GOTH, leading AARON with his CHILD in his arms.]

SECOND GOTH.

Renowned Lucius, from our troops I stray'd

To gaze upon a ruinous monastery;

And as I earnestly did fix mine eye

Upon the wasted building, suddenly

I heard a child cry underneath a wall.

I made unto the noise; when soon I heard

The crying babe controll'd with this discourse:—

'Peace, tawny slave, half me and half thy dam!

Did not thy hue bewray whose brat thou art,

Had nature lent thee but thy mother's look,

Villain, thou mightst have been an emperor:

But where the bull and cow are both milk-white,

They never do beget a coal-black calf.

Peace, villain, peace!'—even thus he rates the babe,—

'For I must bear thee to a trusty Goth;

Who, when he knows thou art the empress' babe,

Will hold thee dearly for thy mother's sake.'

With this, my weapon drawn, I rush'd upon him,

Surpris'd him suddenly, and brought him hither,

To use as you think needful of the man.

LUCIUS.

O worthy Goth, this is the incarnate devil

That robb'd Andronicus of his good hand;

This is the pearl that pleas'd your empress' eye;

And here's the base fruit of his burning lust.—

Say, wall-ey'd slave, whither wouldst thou convey

This growing image of thy fiend-like face?

Why dost not speak? what, deaf? No; not a word?—

A halter, soldiers; hang him on this tree,

And by his side his fruit of bastardy.

AARON.

Touch not the boy,—he is of royal blood.

LUCIUS.

Too like the sire for ever being good.—

First hang the child, that he may see it sprawl,—

A sight to vex the father's soul withal.

Get me a ladder.

        [A ladder brought, which AARON is obliged to ascend.]

AARON.

Lucius, save the child,

And bear it from me to the empress.

If thou do this, I'll show thee wondrous things

That highly may advantage thee to hear:

If thou wilt not, befall what may befall,

I'll speak no more,—but vengeance rot you all!

LUCIUS.

Say on: an if it please me which thou speak'st,

Thy child shall live, and I will see it nourish'd.

AARON.

An if it please thee! why, assure thee, Lucius,

'Twill vex thy soul to hear what I shall speak;

For I must talk of murders, rapes, and massacres,

Acts of black night, abominable deeds,

Complots of mischief, treason, villainies,

Ruthful to hear, yet piteously perform'd:

And this shall all be buried in my death,

Unless thou swear to me my child shall live.

LUCIUS.

Tell on thy mind; I say thy child shall live.

AARON.

Swear that he shall, and then I will begin.

LUCIUS.

Who should I swear by? thou believ'st no god;:

That granted, how canst thou believe an oath?

AARON.

What if I do not? as indeed I do not;

Yet, for I know thou art religious,

And hast a thing within thee called conscience,

With twenty popish tricks and ceremonies

Which I have seen thee careful to observe,

Therefore I urge thy oath;—for that I know

An idiot holds his bauble for a god,

And keeps the oath which by that god he swears;

To that I'll urge him:—therefore thou shalt vow

By that same god,—what god soe'er it be

That thou ador'st and hast in reverence,—

To save my boy, to nourish and bring him up;

Or else I will discover naught to thee.

LUCIUS.

Even by my god I swear to thee I will.

AARON.

First know thou, I begot him on the empress.

LUCIUS.

O most insatiate and luxurious woman!

AARON.

Tut, Lucius, this was but a deed of charity

To that which thou shalt hear of me anon.

'Twas her two sons that murder'd Bassianus;

They cut thy sister's tongue, and ravish'd her,

And cut her hands, and trimm'd her as thou saw'st.

LUCIUS.

O detestable villain! call'st thou that trimming?

AARON.

Why, she was wash'd, and cut, and trimm'd; and 'twas

Trim sport for them which had the doing of it.

LUCIUS.

O barbarous, beastly villains, like thyself!

AARON.

Indeed, I was their tutor to instruct them:

That codding spirit had they from their mother,

As sure a card as ever won the set;

That bloody mind, I think, they learn'd of me,

As true a dog as ever fought at head.

Well, let my deeds be witness of my worth.

I train'd thy brethren to that guileful hole

Where the dead corpse of Bassianus lay:

I wrote the letter that thy father found,

And hid the gold within that letter mention'd,

Confederate with the queen and her two sons:

And what not done, that thou hast cause to rue,

Wherein I had no stroke of mischief in't?

I play'd the cheater for thy father's hand;

And, when I had it, drew myself apart,

And almost broke my heart with extreme laughter:

I pry'd me through the crevice of a wall

When, for his hand, he had his two sons' heads;

Beheld his tears, and laugh'd so heartily

That both mine eyes were rainy like to his:

And when I told the empress of this sport,

She swooned almost at my pleasing tale,

And for my tidings gave me twenty kisses.

GOTH.

What, canst thou say all this and never blush?

AARON.

Ay, like a black dog, as the saying is.

LUCIUS.

Art thou not sorry for these heinous deeds?

AARON.

Ay, that I had not done a thousand more.

Even now I curse the day,—and yet, I think,

Few come within the compass of my curse,—

Wherein I did not some notorious ill:

As, kill a man, or else devise his death;

Ravish a maid, or plot the way to do it;

Accuse some innocent, and forswear myself;

Set deadly enmity between two friends;

Make poor men's cattle stray and break their necks;

Set fire on barns and hay-stacks in the night,

And bid the owners quench them with their tears.

Oft have I digg'd up dead men from their graves,

And set them upright at their dear friends' doors,

Even when their sorrows almost were forgot;

And on their skins, as on the bark of trees,

Have with my knife carved in Roman letters,

'Let not your sorrow die, though I am dead.'

Tut, I have done a thousand dreadful things

As willingly as one would kill a fly;

And nothing grieves me heartily indeed

But that I cannot do ten thousand more.

LUCIUS.

Bring down the devil; for he must not die

So sweet a death as hanging presently.

AARON.

If there be devils, would I were a devil,

To live and burn in everlasting fire,

So I might have your company in hell

But to torment you with my bitter tongue!

133

LUCIUS.

Sirs, stop his mouth, and let him speak no more.

[Enter a GOTH.}

THIRD GOTH.

My lord, there is a messenger from Rome

Desires to be admitted to your presence.

LUCIUS.

Let him come near.

[Enter AEMILIUS.]

Welcome, Aemilius. What's the news from Rome?

AEMILIUS.

Lord Lucius, and you princes of the Goths,

The Roman emperor greets you all by me;

And, for he understands you are in arms,

He craves a parley at your father's house,

Willing you to demand your hostages,

And they shall be immediately deliver'd.

FIRST GOTH.

What says our general?

LUCIUS.

Aemilius, let the emperor give his pledges

Unto my father and my uncle Marcus.

And we will come.—March away.

[Exeunt.]

SCENE II. Rome. Before TITUS'S House.

[Enter TAMORA, DEMETRIUS and CHIRON, disguised.]

TAMORA.

Thus, in this strange and sad habiliment,

I will encounter with Andronicus,

And say I am Revenge, sent from below

To join with him and right his heinous wrongs.

Knock at his study, where they say he keeps

To ruminate strange plots of dire revenge;

Tell him Revenge is come to join with him,

And work confusion on his enemies.

[They knock.]

[Enter TITUS, above.]

TITUS.

Who doth molest my contemplation?

Is it your trick to make me ope the door,

That so my sad decrees may fly away

And all my study be to no effect?

You are deceiv'd: for what I mean to do

See here in bloody lines I have set down;

And what is written shall be executed.

TAMORA.

Titus, I am come to talk with thee.

TITUS.

No, not a word: how can I grace my talk,

Wanting a hand to give it action?

Thou hast the odds of me; therefore no more.

TAMORA.

If thou didst know me, thou wouldst talk with me.

TITUS.

I am not mad; I know thee well enough:

Witness this wretched stump, witness these crimson lines;

Witness these trenches made by grief and care;

Witness the tiring day and heavy night;

Witness all sorrow, that I know thee well

For our proud empress, mighty Tamora:

Is not thy coming for my other hand?

TAMORA.

Know thou, sad man, I am not Tamora;

She is thy enemy and I thy friend:

I am Revenge; sent from the infernal kingdom

To ease the gnawing vulture of thy mind

By working wreakful vengeance on thy foes.

Come down and welcome me to this world's light;

Confer with me of murder and of death:

There's not a hollow cave or lurking-place,

No vast obscurity or misty vale,

Where bloody murder or detested rape

Can couch for fear but I will find them out;

And in their ears tell them my dreadful name,—

Revenge, which makes the foul offender quake.

TITUS.

Art thou Revenge? and art thou sent to me

To be a torment to mine enemies?

TAMORA.

I am; therefore come down and welcome me.

TITUS.

Do me some service ere I come to thee.

Lo, by thy side where Rape and Murder stands;

Now give some surance that thou art Revenge,—

Stab them, or tear them on thy chariot wheels;

And then I'll come and be thy waggoner,

And whirl along with thee about the globe.

Provide thee two proper palfreys, black as jet,

To hale thy vengeful waggon swift away,

And find out murderers in their guilty caves:

And when thy car is loaden with their heads

I will dismount, and by the waggon-wheel

Trot, like a servile footman, all day long,

Even from Hyperion's rising in the east

Until his very downfall in the sea:

And day by day I'll do this heavy task,

So thou destroy Rapine and Murder there.

TAMORA.

These are my ministers, and come with me.

TITUS.

Are they thy ministers? what are they call'd?

TAMORA.

Rapine and Murder; therefore called so

'Cause they take vengeance of such kind of men.

TITUS.

Good Lord, how like the empress' sons they are!

And you the empress! But we worldly men

Have miserable, mad, mistaking eyes.

O sweet Revenge, now do I come to thee;

And, if one arm's embracement will content thee,

I will embrace thee in it by and by.

[Exit from above.]

TAMORA.

This closing with him fits his lunacy:

Whate'er I forge to feed his brain-sick fiits,

Do you uphold and maintain in your speeches,

For now he firmly takes me for Revenge;

And, being credulous in this mad thought,

I'll make him send for Lucius his son;

And whilst I at a banquet hold him sure,

I'll find some cunning practice out of hand

To scatter and disperse the giddy Goths,

Or, at the least, make them his enemies.

See, here he comes, and I must ply my theme.

[Enter TITUS.]

TITUS.

Long have I been forlorn, and all for thee:

Welcome, dread fury, to my woeful house;—

Rapine and Murder, you are welcome too:—

How like the empress and her sons you are!

Well are you fitted, had you but a Moor:

Could not all hell afford you such a devil?—

For well I wot the empress never wags

But in her company there is a Moor;

And, would you represent our queen aright,

It were convenient you had such a devil:

But welcome as you are. What shall we do?

TAMORA.

What wouldst thou have us do, Andronicus?

DEMETRIUS.

Show me a murderer, I'll deal with him.

CHIRON.

Show me a villain that hath done a rape,

And I am sent to be reveng'd on him.

TAMORA.

Show me a thousand that hath done thee wrong,

And I will be revenged on them all.

TITUS.

Look round about the wicked streets of Rome,

And when thou find'st a man that's like thyself,

Good Murder, stab him; he's a murderer.—

Go thou with him; and when it is thy hap

To find another that is like to thee,

Good Rapine, stab him; he is a ravisher.—

Go thou with them; and in the emperor's court

There is a queen, attended by a Moor;

Well mayst thou know her by thine own proportion,

For up and down she doth resemble thee;

I pray thee, do on them some violent death;

They have been violent to me and mine.

TAMORA.

Well hast thou lesson'd us; this shall we do.

But would it please thee, good Andronicus,

To send for Lucius, thy thrice-valiant son,

Who leads towards Rome a band of warlike Goths,

And bid him come and banquet at thy house;

When he is here, even at thy solemn feast,

I will bring in the empress and her sons,

The emperor himself, and all thy foes;

And at thy mercy shall they stoop and kneel,

And on them shalt thou ease thy angry heart.

What says Andronicus to this device?

TITUS.

Marcus, my brother!—'tis sad Titus calls.

[Enter MARCUS.]

Go, gentle Marcus, to thy nephew Lucius;

Thou shalt inquire him out among the Goths:

Bid him repair to me, and bring with him

Some of the chiefest princes of the Goths;

Bid him encamp his soldiers where they are:

Tell him the emperor and the empress too

Feast at my house, and he shall feast with them.

This do thou for my love; and so let him,

As he regards his aged father's life.

MARCUS.

This will I do, and soon return again.

[Exit.]

TAMORA.

Now will I hence about thy business,

And take my ministers along with me.

TITUS.

Nay, nay, let Rape and Murder stay with me,

Or else I'll call my brother back again,

And cleave to no revenge but Lucius.

TAMORA.

[Aside to them.] What say you, boys? will you abide with him,

Whiles I go tell my lord the emperor

How I have govern'd our determin'd jest?

Yield to his humour, smooth and speak him fair,

And tarry with him till I come again.

TITUS.

[Aside.] I knew them all, though they suppose me mad,

And will o'er reach them in their own devices,—

A pair of cursed hell-hounds and their dam.

DEMETRIUS.

Madam, depart at pleasure; leave us here.

TAMORA.

Farewell, Andronicus: Revenge now goes

To lay a complot to betray thy foes.

TITUS.

I know thou dost; and, sweet Revenge, farewell!

[Exit TAMORA.]

CHIRON.

Tell us, old man, how shall we be employ'd?

TITUS.

Tut, I have work enough for you to do.—

Publius, come hither, Caius, and Valentine.

[Enter PUBLIUS and others.]

PUBLIUS.

What is your will?

TITUS.

Know you these two?

PUBLIUS.

The empress' sons, I take them: Chiron, Demetrius.

TITUS.

Fie, Publius, fie! thou art too much deceiv'd,—

The one is Murder, Rape is the other's name;

And therefore bind them, gentle Publius:—

Caius and Valentine, lay hands on them:—

Oft have you heard me wish for such an hour,

And now I find it; therefore bind them sure;

And stop their mouths if they begin to cry.

[Exit. PUBLIUS &c., lay hands on CHIRON and DEMETRIUS.]

CHIRON.

Villains, forbear! we are the empress' sons.

143

PUBLIUS.

And therefore do we what we are commanded.—

Stop close their mouths, let them not speak a word.

Is he sure bound? look that you bind them fast.

[Re-enter TITUS ANDRONICUS, with LAVINIA; he bearing a knife and she a basin.]

TITUS.

Come, come, Lavinia; look, thy foes are bound.—

Sirs, stop their mouths, let them not speak to me;

But let them hear what fearful words I utter.—

O villains, Chiron and Demetrius!

Here stands the spring whom you have stain'd with mud;

This goodly summer with your winter mix'd.

You kill'd her husband; and for that vile fault

Two of her brothers were condemn'd to death,

My hand cut off and made a merry jest;

Both her sweet hands, her tongue, and that, more dear

Than hands or tongue, her spotless chastity,

Inhuman traitors, you constrain'd and forc'd.

What would you say, if I should let you speak?

Villains, for shame you could not beg for grace.

Hark, wretches! how I mean to martyr you.

This one hand yet is left to cut your throats,

Whiles that Lavinia 'tween her stumps doth hold

The basin that receives your guilty blood.

You know your mother means to feast with me,

And calls herself Revenge, and thinks me mad:—

Hark, villains! I will grind your bones to dust,

And with your blood and it I'll make a paste;

And of the paste a coffin I will rear,

And make two pasties of your shameful heads;

And bid that strumpet, your unhallow'd dam,

Like to the earth, swallow her own increase.

This is the feast that I have bid her to,

And this the banquet she shall surfeit on;

For worse than Philomel you us'd my daughter,

And worse than Progne I will be reveng'd:

And now prepare your throats. Lavinia, come

[He cuts their throats.]

Receive the blood: and when that they are dead,

Let me go grind their bones to powder small,

And with this hateful liquor temper it;

And in that paste let their vile heads be bak'd.

Come, come, be every one officious

To make this banquet; which I wish may prove

More stern and bloody than the Centaurs' feast.

So, now bring them in, for I will play the cook,

And see them ready against their mother comes.

[Exeunt, bearing the dead bodies.]

145

SCENE III. Rome. A Pavilion in TITUS'S Gardens, with tables, &c.

[Enter LUCIUS, MARCUS, and GOTHS, with AARON prisoner.]

LUCIUS.

Uncle Marcus, since 'tis my father's mind

That I repair to Rome, I am content.

FIRST GOTH.

And ours with thine, befall what fortune will.

LUCIUS.

Good uncle, take you in this barbarous Moor,

This ravenous tiger, this accursed devil;

Let him receive no sustenance, fetter him,

Till he be brought unto the empress' face

For testimony of her foul proceedings:

And see the ambush of our friends be strong;

I fear the emperor means no good to us.

AARON.

Some devil whisper curses in my ear,

And prompt me that my tongue may utter forth

The venomous malice of my swelling heart!

LUCIUS.

Away, inhuman dog, unhallowed slave!—

Sirs, help our uncle to convey him in.—

[Exeunt GOTHS with AARON. Flourish within. The trumpets show the emperor is at hand.]

[Enter SATURNINUS and TAMORA, with AEMILIUS, Tribunes, Senators, and others.]

SATURNINUS.

What, hath the firmament more suns than one?

LUCIUS.

What boots it thee to call thyself the sun?

MARCUS.

Rome's emperor, and nephew, break the parle;

These quarrels must be quietly debated.

The feast is ready, which the careful Titus

Hath ordain'd to an honourable end,

For peace, for love, for league, and good to Rome:

Please you, therefore, draw nigh and take your places.

SATURNINUS.

Marcus, we will.

[Hautboys sound. The company sit at table.]

[Enter TITUS, dressed like a cook, LAVINIA, valed, YOUNG LUCIUS, and others. TITUS places the dishes on the table.]

TITUS.

Welcome, my lord; welcome, dread queen;

Welcome, ye warlike Goths; welcome, Lucius;

And welcome all: although the cheer be poor,

'Twill fill your stomachs; please you eat of it.

SATURNINUS.

Why art thou thus attir'd, Andronicus?

TITUS.

Because I would be sure to have all well

To entertain your highness and your empress.

TAMORA.

We are beholden to you, good Andronicus.

TITUS.

An if your highness knew my heart, you were.

My lord the emperor, resolve me this:

Was it well done of rash Virginius

To slay his daughter with his own right hand,

Because she was enforc'd, stain'd, and deflower'd?

SATURNINUS.

It was, Andronicus.

TITUS.

Your reason, mighty lord.

SATURNINUS.

Because the girl should not survive her shame,

And by her presence still renew his sorrows.

TITUS.

A reason mighty, strong, and effectual;

A pattern, precedent, and lively warrant

For me, most wretched, to perform the like:—

Die, die, Lavinia, and thy shame with thee;

[Kills LAVINIA.]

And with thy shame thy father's sorrow die!

SATURNINUS.

What hast thou done, unnatural and unkind?

TITUS.

Kill'd her for whom my tears have made me blind.

I am as woeful as Virginius was,

And have a thousand times more cause than he

To do this outrage;—and it now is done.

SATURNINUS.

What, was she ravish'd? tell who did the deed.

TITUS.

Will't please you eat? will't please your highness feed?

TAMORA.

Why hast thou slain thine only daughter thus?

TITUS.

Not I; 'twas Chiron and Demetrius:

They ravish'd her, and cut away her tongue;

And they, 'twas they, that did her all this wrong.

SATURNINUS.

Go, fetch them hither to us presently.

TITUS.

Why, there they are, both baked in that pie,

Whereof their mother daintily hath fed,

Eating the flesh that she herself hath bred.

'Tis true, 'tis true; witness my knife's sharp point.

[Kills Tamora.]

SATURNINUS.

Die, frantic wretch, for this accursed deed!

[Kills TITUS.]

LUCIUS.

Can the son's eye behold his father bleed?

There's meed for meed, death for a deadly deed.

[Kills SATURNINUS. A great tumult. LUCIUS, MARCUS, and their partisans, ascend the steps before TITUS'S house.]

MARCUS.

You sad-fac'd men, people and sons of Rome,

By uproar sever'd, as a flight of fowl

Scatter'd by winds and high tempestuous gusts,

O, let me teach you how to knit again

This scattered corn into one mutual sheaf,

These broken limbs again into one body:

Lest Rome herself be bane unto herself,

And she whom mighty kingdoms court'sy to,

Like a forlorn and desperate castaway,

Do shameful execution on herself.

But if my frosty signs and chaps of age,

Grave witnesses of true experience,

Cannot induce you to attend my words,—

Speak, Rome's dear friend,[to Lucius]: as erst our ancestor,

When with his solemn tongue he did discourse

To love-sick Dido's sad attending ear

The story of that baleful burning night,

When subtle Greeks surpris'd King Priam's Troy,—

Tell us what Sinon hath bewitch'd our ears,

Or who hath brought the fatal engine in

That gives our Troy, our Rome, the civil wound.

My heart is not compact of flint nor steel;

Nor can I utter all our bitter grief,

But floods of tears will drown my oratory

And break my very utterance, even in the time

When it should move you to attend me most,

Lending your kind commiseration.

Here is a captain, let him tell the tale;

Your hearts will throb and weep to hear him speak.

LUCIUS.

Then, noble auditory, be it known to you

That cursed Chiron and Demetrius

Were they that murdered our emperor's brother;

And they it were that ravished our sister:

For their fell faults our brothers were beheaded;

Our father's tears despis'd, and basely cozen'd

Of that true hand that fought Rome's quarrel out

And sent her enemies unto the grave.

Lastly, myself unkindly banished,

The gates shut on me, and turn'd weeping out,

To beg relief among Rome's enemies;

Who drown'd their enmity in my true tears,

And op'd their arms to embrace me as a friend:

I am the turned-forth, be it known to you,

That have preserv'd her welfare in my blood;

And from her bosom took the enemy's point,

Sheathing the steel in my adventurous body.

Alas! you know I am no vaunter, I;

My scars can witness, dumb although they are,

That my report is just and full of truth.

But, soft! methinks I do digress too much,

Citing my worthless praise: O, pardon me;

For when no friends are by, men praise themselves.

MARCUS.

Now is my turn to speak. Behold the child.

              [Pointing to the CHILD in an Attendant's arms.]

Of this was Tamora delivered;

The issue of an irreligious Moor,

Chief architect and plotter of these woes:

The villain is alive in Titus' house,

Damn'd as he is, to witness this is true.

Now judge what cause had Titus to revenge

These wrongs unspeakable, past patience,

Or more than any living man could bear.

Now have you heard the truth, what say you, Romans?

Have we done aught amiss,—show us wherein,

And, from the place where you behold us now,

The poor remainder of Andronici

Will, hand in hand, all headlong cast us down,

And on the ragged stones beat forth our brains,

And make a mutual closure of our house.

Speak, Romans, speak; and if you say we shall,

Lo, hand in hand, Lucius and I will fall.

AEMILIUS.

Come, come, thou reverend man of Rome,

And bring our emperor gently in thy hand,

Lucius our emperor; for well I know

The common voice do cry it shall be so.

ROMANS.

[Several speak.] Lucius, all hail, Rome's royal emperor!

MARCUS.

Go, go into old Titus' sorrowful house,

[To attendants, who go into the house.]

And hither hale that misbelieving Moor

To be adjudg'd some direful slaughtering death,

As punishment for his most wicked life.

[LUCIUS, MARCUS, &c. descend.]

ROMANS.

[Several speak.] Lucius, all hail, Rome's gracious governor!

LUCIUS.

Thanks, gentle Romans: may I govern so

To heal Rome's harms and wipe away her woe!

But, gentle people, give me aim awhile,—

For nature puts me to a heavy task:—

Stand all aloof;—but, uncle, draw you near,

To shed obsequious tears upon this trunk.—

O, take this warm kiss on thy pale cold lips.

[Kisses TITUS.]

These sorrowful drops upon thy blood-stain'd face,

The last true duties of thy noble son!

MARCUS.

Tear for tear and loving kiss for kiss

Thy brother Marcus tenders on thy lips:

O, were the sum of these that I should pay

Countless and infinite, yet would I pay them!

LUCIUS.

Come hither, boy; come, come, and learn of us

To melt in showers: thy grandsire lov'd thee well:

Many a time he danc'd thee on his knee,

Sung thee asleep, his loving breast thy pillow;

Many a matter hath he told to thee,

Meet and agreeing with thine infancy;

In that respect, then, like a loving child,

Shed yet some small drops from thy tender spring,

Because kind nature doth require it so:

Friends should associate friends in grief and woe:

Bid him farewell; commit him to the grave;

Do him that kindness, and take leave of him.

YOUNG LUCIUS.

O grandsire, grandsire! even with all my heart

Would I were dead, so you did live again!—

O Lord, I cannot speak to him for weeping;

My tears will choke me, if I ope my mouth.

                    [Re-enter attendants with AARON.]

AEMILIUS.

You sad Andronici, have done with woes:

Give sentence on the execrable wretch,

That hath been breeder of these dire events.

LUCIUS.

Set him breast-deep in earth, and famish him;

There let him stand and rave and cry for food:

If any one relieves or pities him,

For the offence he dies. This is our doom:

Some stay to see him fasten'd in the earth.

AARON.

Ah, why should wrath be mute and fury dumb?

I am no baby, I, that with base prayers

I should repent the evils I have done:

Ten thousand worse than ever yet I did

Would I perform, if I might have my will:

If one good deed in all my life I did,

I do repent it from my very soul.

LUCIUS.

Some loving friends convey the emperor hence,

And give him burial in his father's grave:

My father and Lavinia shall forthwith

Be closed in our household's monument.

As for that ravenous tiger, Tamora,

No funeral rite, nor man in mournful weeds,

No mournful bell shall ring her burial;

But throw her forth to beasts and birds of prey:

Her life was beast-like and devoid of pity;

And, being so, shall have like want of pity.

See justice done on Aaron, that damn'd Moor,

By whom our heavy haps had their beginning:

Then, afterwards, to order well the state,

That like events may ne'er it ruinate.

[Exeunt.]

ROMEO AND JULIET

Dramatis Personæ

ESCALUS, Prince of Verona.

MERCUTIO, kinsman to the Prince, and friend to Romeo.

PARIS, a young Nobleman, kinsman to the Prince.

Page to Paris.

MONTAGUE, head of a Veronese family at feud with the Capulets.

LADY MONTAGUE, wife to Montague.

ROMEO, son to Montague.

BENVOLIO, nephew to Montague, and friend to Romeo.

ABRAM, servant to Montague.

BALTHASAR, servant to Romeo.

CAPULET, head of a Veronese family at feud with the Montagues.

LADY CAPULET, wife to Capulet.

JULIET, daughter to Capulet.

TYBALT, nephew to Lady Capulet.

CAPULET'S COUSIN, an old man.

NURSE to Juliet.

PETER, servant to Juliet's Nurse.

SAMPSON, servant to Capulet.

GREGORY, servant to Capulet.

Servants.

FRIAR LAWRENCE, a Franciscan.

FRIAR JOHN, of the same Order.

An Apothecary.

CHORUS.

Three Musicians.

An Officer.

Citizens of Verona; several Men and Women, relations to both houses; Maskers, Guards, Watchmen and Attendants.

SCENE. During the greater part of the Play in Verona; once, in the Fifth Act, at Mantua.

THE PROLOGUE

Enter Chorus.

CHORUS.

Two households, both alike in dignity,

In fair Verona, where we lay our scene,

From ancient grudge break to new mutiny,

Where civil blood makes civil hands unclean.

From forth the fatal loins of these two foes

A pair of star-cross'd lovers take their life;

Whose misadventur'd piteous overthrows

Doth with their death bury their parents' strife.

The fearful passage of their death-mark'd love,

And the continuance of their parents' rage,

Which, but their children's end, nought could remove,

Is now the two hours' traffic of our stage;

The which, if you with patient ears attend,

What here shall miss, our toil shall strive to mend.

[Exit.]

ACT I

SCENE I. A public place.

Enter Sampson and Gregory armed with swords and bucklers.

SAMPSON.

Gregory, on my word, we'll not carry coals.

GREGORY.

No, for then we should be colliers.

SAMPSON.

I mean, if we be in choler, we'll draw.

GREGORY.

Ay, while you live, draw your neck out o' the collar.

SAMPSON.

I strike quickly, being moved.

GREGORY.

But thou art not quickly moved to strike.

SAMPSON.

A dog of the house of Montague moves me.

GREGORY.

To move is to stir; and to be valiant is to stand: therefore, if thou art moved, thou runn'st away.

SAMPSON.

A dog of that house shall move me to stand.

I will take the wall of any man or maid of Montague's.

GREGORY.

That shows thee a weak slave, for the weakest goes to the wall.

SAMPSON.

True, and therefore women, being the weaker vessels, are ever thrust to the wall: therefore I will push Montague's men from the wall, and thrust his maids to the wall.

GREGORY.

The quarrel is between our masters and us their men.

SAMPSON.

'Tis all one, I will show myself a tyrant: when I have fought with the men I will be civil with the maids, I will cut off their heads.

GREGORY.

The heads of the maids?

SAMPSON.

Ay, the heads of the maids, or their maidenheads; take it in what sense thou wilt.

GREGORY.

They must take it in sense that feel it.

SAMPSON.

Me they shall feel while I am able to stand: and 'tis known I am a pretty piece of flesh.

GREGORY.

'Tis well thou art not fish; if thou hadst, thou hadst been poor John.

Draw thy tool; here comes of the house of Montagues.

Enter Abram and Balthasar.

SAMPSON.

My naked weapon is out: quarrel, I will back thee.

GREGORY.

How? Turn thy back and run?

SAMPSON.

Fear me not.

GREGORY.

No, marry; I fear thee!

SAMPSON.

Let us take the law of our sides; let them begin.

GREGORY.

I will frown as I pass by, and let them take it as they list.

SAMPSON.

Nay, as they dare. I will bite my thumb at them, which is disgrace to them if they bear it.

ABRAM.

Do you bite your thumb at us, sir?

SAMPSON.

I do bite my thumb, sir.

ABRAM.

Do you bite your thumb at us, sir?

SAMPSON.

Is the law of our side if I say ay?

GREGORY.

No.

SAMPSON.

No sir, I do not bite my thumb at you, sir; but I bite my thumb, sir.

GREGORY.

Do you quarrel, sir?

ABRAM.

Quarrel, sir? No, sir.

SAMPSON.

But if you do, sir, am for you. I serve as good a man as you.

ABRAM.

No better.

SAMPSON.

Well, sir.

Enter Benvolio.

GREGORY.

Say better; here comes one of my master's kinsmen.

SAMPSON.

Yes, better, sir.

ABRAM.

You lie.

SAMPSON.

Draw, if you be men. Gregory, remember thy washing blow.

[They fight.]

BENVOLIO.

Part, fools! put up your swords, you know not what you do.

[Beats down their swords.]

Enter Tybalt.

TYBALT.

What, art thou drawn among these heartless hinds?

Turn thee Benvolio, look upon thy death.

BENVOLIO.

I do but keep the peace, put up thy sword,

Or manage it to part these men with me.

TYBALT.

What, drawn, and talk of peace? I hate the word

As I hate hell, all Montagues, and thee:

Have at thee, coward.

[They fight.]

Enter three or four Citizens with clubs.

FIRST CITIZEN.

Clubs, bills and partisans! Strike! Beat them down!

Down with the Capulets! Down with the Montagues!

Enter Capulet in his gown, and Lady Capulet.

CAPULET.

What noise is this? Give me my long sword, ho!

LADY CAPULET.

A crutch, a crutch! Why call you for a sword?

CAPULET.

My sword, I say! Old Montague is come,

And flourishes his blade in spite of me.

Enter Montague and his Lady Montague.

MONTAGUE.

Thou villain Capulet! Hold me not, let me go.

LADY MONTAGUE.

Thou shalt not stir one foot to seek a foe.

Enter Prince Escalus, with Attendants.

PRINCE.

Rebellious subjects, enemies to peace,

Profaners of this neighbour-stained steel,—

Will they not hear? What, ho! You men, you beasts,

That quench the fire of your pernicious rage

With purple fountains issuing from your veins,

On pain of torture, from those bloody hands

Throw your mistemper'd weapons to the ground

And hear the sentence of your moved prince.

Three civil brawls, bred of an airy word,

By thee, old Capulet, and Montague,

Have thrice disturb'd the quiet of our streets,

And made Verona's ancient citizens

Cast by their grave beseeming ornaments,

To wield old partisans, in hands as old,

Canker'd with peace, to part your canker'd hate.

If ever you disturb our streets again,

Your lives shall pay the forfeit of the peace.

For this time all the rest depart away:

You, Capulet, shall go along with me,

And Montague, come you this afternoon,

To know our farther pleasure in this case,

To old Free-town, our common judgement-place.

Once more, on pain of death, all men depart.

[Exeunt Prince and Attendants; Capulet, Lady Capulet, Tybalt,
Citizens and Servants.]

MONTAGUE.

Who set this ancient quarrel new abroach?

Speak, nephew, were you by when it began?

BENVOLIO.

Here were the servants of your adversary

And yours, close fighting ere I did approach.

I drew to part them, in the instant came

The fiery Tybalt, with his sword prepar'd,

Which, as he breath'd defiance to my ears,

He swung about his head, and cut the winds,

Who nothing hurt withal, hiss'd him in scorn.

While we were interchanging thrusts and blows

Came more and more, and fought on part and part,

Till the Prince came, who parted either part.

LADY MONTAGUE.

O where is Romeo, saw you him today?

Right glad I am he was not at this fray.

BENVOLIO.

Madam, an hour before the worshipp'd sun

Peer'd forth the golden window of the east,

A troubled mind drave me to walk abroad,

Where underneath the grove of sycamore

That westward rooteth from this city side,

So early walking did I see your son.

Towards him I made, but he was ware of me,

And stole into the covert of the wood.

I, measuring his affections by my own,

Which then most sought where most might not be found,

Being one too many by my weary self,

Pursu'd my humour, not pursuing his,

And gladly shunn'd who gladly fled from me.

MONTAGUE.

Many a morning hath he there been seen,

With tears augmenting the fresh morning's dew,

Adding to clouds more clouds with his deep sighs;

But all so soon as the all-cheering sun

Should in the farthest east begin to draw

The shady curtains from Aurora's bed,

Away from light steals home my heavy son,

And private in his chamber pens himself,

Shuts up his windows, locks fair daylight out

And makes himself an artificial night.

Black and portentous must this humour prove,

Unless good counsel may the cause remove.

BENVOLIO.

My noble uncle, do you know the cause?

MONTAGUE.

I neither know it nor can learn of him.

BENVOLIO.

Have you importun'd him by any means?

MONTAGUE.

Both by myself and many other friends;

But he, his own affections' counsellor,

Is to himself—I will not say how true—

But to himself so secret and so close,

So far from sounding and discovery,

As is the bud bit with an envious worm

Ere he can spread his sweet leaves to the air,

Or dedicate his beauty to the sun.

Could we but learn from whence his sorrows grow,

We would as willingly give cure as know.

Enter Romeo.

BENVOLIO.

See, where he comes. So please you step aside;

I'll know his grievance or be much denied.

MONTAGUE.

I would thou wert so happy by thy stay

To hear true shrift. Come, madam, let's away,

[Exeunt Montague and Lady Montague.]

BENVOLIO.

Good morrow, cousin.

ROMEO.

Is the day so young?

BENVOLIO.

But new struck nine.

ROMEO.

Ay me, sad hours seem long.

Was that my father that went hence so fast?

BENVOLIO.

It was. What sadness lengthens Romeo's hours?

ROMEO.

Not having that which, having, makes them short.

BENVOLIO.

In love?

ROMEO.

Out.

BENVOLIO.

Of love?

ROMEO.

Out of her favour where I am in love.

BENVOLIO.

Alas that love so gentle in his view,

Should be so tyrannous and rough in proof.

ROMEO.

Alas that love, whose view is muffled still,

Should, without eyes, see pathways to his will!

Where shall we dine? O me! What fray was here?

Yet tell me not, for I have heard it all.

Here's much to do with hate, but more with love:

Why, then, O brawling love! O loving hate!

O anything, of nothing first create!

O heavy lightness! serious vanity!

Misshapen chaos of well-seeming forms!

Feather of lead, bright smoke, cold fire, sick health!

Still-waking sleep, that is not what it is!

This love feel I, that feel no love in this.

Dost thou not laugh?

BENVOLIO.

No coz, I rather weep.

ROMEO.

Good heart, at what?

BENVOLIO.

At thy good heart's oppression.

ROMEO.

Why such is love's transgression.

Griefs of mine own lie heavy in my breast,

Which thou wilt propagate to have it prest

With more of thine. This love that thou hast shown

Doth add more grief to too much of mine own.

Love is a smoke made with the fume of sighs;

Being purg'd, a fire sparkling in lovers' eyes;

Being vex'd, a sea nourish'd with lovers' tears:

What is it else? A madness most discreet,

A choking gall, and a preserving sweet.

Farewell, my coz.

[Going.]

BENVOLIO.

Soft! I will go along:

And if you leave me so, you do me wrong.

ROMEO.

Tut! I have lost myself; I am not here.

This is not Romeo, he's some other where.

BENVOLIO.

Tell me in sadness who is that you love?

ROMEO.

What, shall I groan and tell thee?

BENVOLIO.

Groan! Why, no; but sadly tell me who.

ROMEO.

Bid a sick man in sadness make his will,

A word ill urg'd to one that is so ill.

In sadness, cousin, I do love a woman.

BENVOLIO.

I aim'd so near when I suppos'd you lov'd.

ROMEO.

A right good markman, and she's fair I love.

BENVOLIO.

A right fair mark, fair coz, is soonest hit.

ROMEO.

Well, in that hit you miss: she'll not be hit

With Cupid's arrow, she hath Dian's wit;

And in strong proof of chastity well arm'd,

From love's weak childish bow she lives uncharm'd.

She will not stay the siege of loving terms

Nor bide th'encounter of assailing eyes,

Nor ope her lap to saint-seducing gold:

O she's rich in beauty, only poor

That when she dies, with beauty dies her store.

BENVOLIO.

Then she hath sworn that she will still live chaste?

ROMEO.

She hath, and in that sparing makes huge waste;

For beauty starv'd with her severity,

Cuts beauty off from all posterity.

She is too fair, too wise; wisely too fair,

To merit bliss by making me despair.

She hath forsworn to love, and in that vow

Do I live dead, that live to tell it now.

BENVOLIO.

Be rul'd by me, forget to think of her.

ROMEO.

O teach me how I should forget to think.

BENVOLIO.

By giving liberty unto thine eyes;

Examine other beauties.

ROMEO.

'Tis the way

To call hers, exquisite, in question more.

These happy masks that kiss fair ladies' brows,

Being black, puts us in mind they hide the fair;

He that is strucken blind cannot forget

The precious treasure of his eyesight lost.

Show me a mistress that is passing fair,

What doth her beauty serve but as a note

Where I may read who pass'd that passing fair?

Farewell, thou canst not teach me to forget.

BENVOLIO.

I'll pay that doctrine, or else die in debt.

[Exeunt.]

SCENE II. A Street.

Enter Capulet, Paris and Servant.

CAPULET.

But Montague is bound as well as I,

In penalty alike; and 'tis not hard, I think,

For men so old as we to keep the peace.

PARIS.

Of honourable reckoning are you both,

And pity 'tis you liv'd at odds so long.

But now my lord, what say you to my suit?

CAPULET.

But saying o'er what I have said before.

My child is yet a stranger in the world,

She hath not seen the change of fourteen years;

Let two more summers wither in their pride

Ere we may think her ripe to be a bride.

PARIS.

Younger than she are happy mothers made.

CAPULET.

And too soon marr'd are those so early made.

The earth hath swallowed all my hopes but she,

She is the hopeful lady of my earth:

But woo her, gentle Paris, get her heart,

My will to her consent is but a part;

And she agree, within her scope of choice

Lies my consent and fair according voice.

This night I hold an old accustom'd feast,

Whereto I have invited many a guest,

Such as I love, and you among the store,

One more, most welcome, makes my number more.

At my poor house look to behold this night

Earth-treading stars that make dark heaven light:

Such comfort as do lusty young men feel

When well apparell'd April on the heel

Of limping winter treads, even such delight

Among fresh female buds shall you this night

Inherit at my house. Hear all, all see,

And like her most whose merit most shall be:

Which, on more view of many, mine, being one,

May stand in number, though in reckoning none.

Come, go with me. Go, sirrah, trudge about

Through fair Verona; find those persons out

Whose names are written there, [gives a paper] and to them say,

My house and welcome on their pleasure stay.

                              [Exeunt Capulet and Paris.]

SERVANT.

Find them out whose names are written here! It is written that the shoemaker should meddle with his yard and the tailor with his last, the fisher with his pencil, and the painter with his nets; but I am sent to find those persons whose names are here writ, and can never find what names the writing person hath here writ. I must to the learned. In good time!

Enter Benvolio and Romeo.

BENVOLIO.

Tut, man, one fire burns out another's burning,

One pain is lessen'd by another's anguish;

Turn giddy, and be holp by backward turning;

One desperate grief cures with another's languish:

Take thou some new infection to thy eye,

And the rank poison of the old will die.

ROMEO.

Your plantain leaf is excellent for that.

BENVOLIO.

For what, I pray thee?

ROMEO.

For your broken shin.

BENVOLIO.

Why, Romeo, art thou mad?

ROMEO.

Not mad, but bound more than a madman is:

Shut up in prison, kept without my food,

Whipp'd and tormented and—God-den, good fellow.

SERVANT.

God gi' go-den. I pray, sir, can you read?

ROMEO.

Ay, mine own fortune in my misery.

SERVANT.

Perhaps you have learned it without book.

But I pray, can you read anything you see?

ROMEO.

Ay, If I know the letters and the language.

SERVANT.

Ye say honestly, rest you merry!

ROMEO.

Stay, fellow; I can read.

[He reads the letter.]

Signior Martino and his wife and daughters;

County Anselmo and his beauteous sisters;

The lady widow of Utruvio;

Signior Placentio and his lovely nieces;

Mercutio and his brother Valentine;

Mine uncle Capulet, his wife, and daughters;

My fair niece Rosaline and Livia;

Signior Valentio and his cousin Tybalt;

Lucio and the lively Helena.

A fair assembly. [Gives back the paper] Whither should they come?

SERVANT.

Up.

ROMEO.

Whither to supper?

SERVANT.

To our house.

ROMEO.

Whose house?

SERVANT.

My master's.

ROMEO.

Indeed I should have ask'd you that before.

SERVANT.

Now I'll tell you without asking. My master is the great rich Capulet, and if you be not of the house of Montagues, I pray come and crush a cup of wine. Rest you merry.

[Exit.]

BENVOLIO.

At this same ancient feast of Capulet's

Sups the fair Rosaline whom thou so lov'st;

With all the admired beauties of Verona.

Go thither and with unattainted eye,

Compare her face with some that I shall show,

And I will make thee think thy swan a crow.

182

ROMEO.

When the devout religion of mine eye

Maintains such falsehood, then turn tears to fire;

And these who, often drown'd, could never die,

Transparent heretics, be burnt for liars.

One fairer than my love? The all-seeing sun

Ne'er saw her match since first the world begun.

BENVOLIO.

Tut, you saw her fair, none else being by,

Herself pois'd with herself in either eye:

But in that crystal scales let there be weigh'd

Your lady's love against some other maid

That I will show you shining at this feast,

And she shall scant show well that now shows best.

ROMEO.

I'll go along, no such sight to be shown,

But to rejoice in splendour of my own.

[Exeunt.]

SCENE III. Room in Capulet's House.

Enter Lady Capulet and Nurse.

LADY CAPULET.

Nurse, where's my daughter? Call her forth to me.

NURSE.

Now, by my maidenhead, at twelve year old,

I bade her come. What, lamb! What ladybird!

God forbid! Where's this girl? What, Juliet!

Enter Juliet.

JULIET.

How now, who calls?

NURSE.

Your mother.

JULIET.

Madam, I am here. What is your will?

LADY CAPULET.

This is the matter. Nurse, give leave awhile,

We must talk in secret. Nurse, come back again,

I have remember'd me, thou's hear our counsel.

Thou knowest my daughter's of a pretty age.

NURSE.

Faith, I can tell her age unto an hour.

LADY CAPULET.

She's not fourteen.

NURSE.

I'll lay fourteen of my teeth,

And yet, to my teen be it spoken, I have but four,

She is not fourteen. How long is it now

To Lammas-tide?

LADY CAPULET.

A fortnight and odd days.

NURSE.

Even or odd, of all days in the year,

Come Lammas Eve at night shall she be fourteen.

Susan and she,—God rest all Christian souls!—

Were of an age. Well, Susan is with God;

She was too good for me. But as I said,

On Lammas Eve at night shall she be fourteen;

That shall she, marry; I remember it well.

'Tis since the earthquake now eleven years;

And she was wean'd,—I never shall forget it—,

Of all the days of the year, upon that day:

For I had then laid wormwood to my dug,

Sitting in the sun under the dovehouse wall;

My lord and you were then at Mantua:

Nay, I do bear a brain. But as I said,

When it did taste the wormwood on the nipple

Of my dug and felt it bitter, pretty fool,

To see it tetchy, and fall out with the dug!

Shake, quoth the dovehouse: 'twas no need, I trow,

To bid me trudge.

And since that time it is eleven years;

For then she could stand alone; nay, by th'rood

She could have run and waddled all about;

For even the day before she broke her brow,

And then my husband,—God be with his soul!

A was a merry man,—took up the child:

'Yea,' quoth he, 'dost thou fall upon thy face?

Thou wilt fall backward when thou hast more wit;

Wilt thou not, Jule?' and, by my holidame,

The pretty wretch left crying, and said 'Ay'.

To see now how a jest shall come about.

I warrant, and I should live a thousand years,

I never should forget it. 'Wilt thou not, Jule?' quoth he;

And, pretty fool, it stinted, and said 'Ay.'

LADY CAPULET.

Enough of this; I pray thee hold thy peace.

NURSE.

Yes, madam, yet I cannot choose but laugh,

To think it should leave crying, and say 'Ay';

And yet I warrant it had upon it brow

A bump as big as a young cockerel's stone;

A perilous knock, and it cried bitterly.

'Yea,' quoth my husband, 'fall'st upon thy face?

Thou wilt fall backward when thou comest to age;

Wilt thou not, Jule?' it stinted, and said 'Ay'.

JULIET.

And stint thou too, I pray thee, Nurse, say I.

NURSE.

Peace, I have done. God mark thee to his grace

Thou wast the prettiest babe that e'er I nurs'd:

And I might live to see thee married once, I have my wish.

LADY CAPULET.

Marry, that marry is the very theme

I came to talk of. Tell me, daughter Juliet,

How stands your disposition to be married?

JULIET.

It is an honour that I dream not of.

NURSE.

An honour! Were not I thine only nurse,

I would say thou hadst suck'd wisdom from thy teat.

LADY CAPULET.

Well, think of marriage now: younger than you,

Here in Verona, ladies of esteem,

Are made already mothers. By my count

I was your mother much upon these years

That you are now a maid. Thus, then, in brief;

The valiant Paris seeks you for his love.

NURSE.

A man, young lady! Lady, such a man

As all the world—why he's a man of wax.

LADY CAPULET.

Verona's summer hath not such a flower.

NURSE.

Nay, he's a flower, in faith a very flower.

LADY CAPULET.

What say you, can you love the gentleman?

This night you shall behold him at our feast;

Read o'er the volume of young Paris' face,

And find delight writ there with beauty's pen.

Examine every married lineament,

And see how one another lends content;

And what obscur'd in this fair volume lies,

Find written in the margent of his eyes.

This precious book of love, this unbound lover,

To beautify him, only lacks a cover:

The fish lives in the sea; and 'tis much pride

For fair without the fair within to hide.

That book in many's eyes doth share the glory,

That in gold clasps locks in the golden story;

So shall you share all that he doth possess,

By having him, making yourself no less.

NURSE.

No less, nay bigger. Women grow by men.

LADY CAPULET.

Speak briefly, can you like of Paris' love?

JULIET.

I'll look to like, if looking liking move:

But no more deep will I endart mine eye

Than your consent gives strength to make it fly.

Enter a Servant.

SERVANT.

Madam, the guests are come, supper served up, you called, my young lady asked for, the Nurse cursed in the pantry, and everything in extremity. I must hence to wait, I beseech you follow straight.

LADY CAPULET.

We follow thee.

[Exit Servant.]

189

Juliet, the County stays.

NURSE.

Go, girl, seek happy nights to happy days.

[Exeunt.]

SCENE IV. A Street.

Enter Romeo, Mercutio, Benvolio, with five or six Maskers; Torch-bearers and others.

ROMEO.

What, shall this speech be spoke for our excuse?

Or shall we on without apology?

BENVOLIO.

The date is out of such prolixity:

We'll have no Cupid hoodwink'd with a scarf,

Bearing a Tartar's painted bow of lath,

Scaring the ladies like a crow-keeper;

Nor no without-book prologue, faintly spoke

After the prompter, for our entrance:

But let them measure us by what they will,

We'll measure them a measure, and be gone.

ROMEO.

Give me a torch, I am not for this ambling;

Being but heavy I will bear the light.

MERCUTIO.

Nay, gentle Romeo, we must have you dance.

ROMEO.

Not I, believe me, you have dancing shoes,

With nimble soles, I have a soul of lead

So stakes me to the ground I cannot move.

MERCUTIO.

You are a lover, borrow Cupid's wings,

And soar with them above a common bound.

ROMEO.

I am too sore enpierced with his shaft

To soar with his light feathers, and so bound,

I cannot bound a pitch above dull woe.

Under love's heavy burden do I sink.

MERCUTIO.

And, to sink in it, should you burden love;

Too great oppression for a tender thing.

ROMEO.

Is love a tender thing? It is too rough,

Too rude, too boisterous; and it pricks like thorn.

MERCUTIO.

If love be rough with you, be rough with love;

Prick love for pricking, and you beat love down.

Give me a case to put my visage in: [Putting on a mask.]

A visor for a visor. What care I

What curious eye doth quote deformities?

Here are the beetle-brows shall blush for me.

BENVOLIO.

Come, knock and enter; and no sooner in

But every man betake him to his legs.

ROMEO.

A torch for me: let wantons, light of heart,

Tickle the senseless rushes with their heels;

For I am proverb'd with a grandsire phrase,

I'll be a candle-holder and look on,

The game was ne'er so fair, and I am done.

MERCUTIO.

Tut, dun's the mouse, the constable's own word:

If thou art dun, we'll draw thee from the mire

Or save your reverence love, wherein thou stickest

Up to the ears. Come, we burn daylight, ho.

ROMEO.

Nay, that's not so.

MERCUTIO.

I mean sir, in delay

We waste our lights in vain, light lights by day.

Take our good meaning, for our judgment sits

Five times in that ere once in our five wits.

ROMEO.

And we mean well in going to this mask;

But 'tis no wit to go.

MERCUTIO.

Why, may one ask?

ROMEO.

I dreamt a dream tonight.

MERCUTIO.

And so did I.

ROMEO.

Well what was yours?

MERCUTIO.

That dreamers often lie.

ROMEO.

In bed asleep, while they do dream things true.

MERCUTIO.

O, then, I see Queen Mab hath been with you.

She is the fairies' midwife, and she comes

In shape no bigger than an agate-stone

On the fore-finger of an alderman,

Drawn with a team of little atomies

Over men's noses as they lie asleep:

Her waggon-spokes made of long spinners' legs;

The cover, of the wings of grasshoppers;

Her traces, of the smallest spider's web;

The collars, of the moonshine's watery beams;

Her whip of cricket's bone; the lash, of film;

Her waggoner, a small grey-coated gnat,

Not half so big as a round little worm

Prick'd from the lazy finger of a maid:

Her chariot is an empty hazelnut,

Made by the joiner squirrel or old grub,

Time out o' mind the fairies' coachmakers.

And in this state she gallops night by night

Through lovers' brains, and then they dream of love;

O'er courtiers' knees, that dream on curtsies straight;

O'er lawyers' fingers, who straight dream on fees;

O'er ladies' lips, who straight on kisses dream,

Which oft the angry Mab with blisters plagues,

Because their breaths with sweetmeats tainted are:

Sometime she gallops o'er a courtier's nose,

And then dreams he of smelling out a suit;

And sometime comes she with a tithe-pig's tail,

Tickling a parson's nose as a lies asleep,

Then dreams he of another benefice:

Sometime she driveth o'er a soldier's neck,

And then dreams he of cutting foreign throats,

Of breaches, ambuscados, Spanish blades,

Of healths five fathom deep; and then anon

Drums in his ear, at which he starts and wakes;

And, being thus frighted, swears a prayer or two,

And sleeps again. This is that very Mab

That plats the manes of horses in the night;

And bakes the elf-locks in foul sluttish hairs,

Which, once untangled, much misfortune bodes:

This is the hag, when maids lie on their backs,

That presses them, and learns them first to bear,

Making them women of good carriage:

This is she,—

ROMEO.

Peace, peace, Mercutio, peace,

Thou talk'st of nothing.

MERCUTIO.

True, I talk of dreams,

Which are the children of an idle brain,

Begot of nothing but vain fantasy,

Which is as thin of substance as the air,

And more inconstant than the wind, who wooes

Even now the frozen bosom of the north,

And, being anger'd, puffs away from thence,

Turning his side to the dew-dropping south.

BENVOLIO.

This wind you talk of blows us from ourselves:

Supper is done, and we shall come too late.

ROMEO.

I fear too early: for my mind misgives

Some consequence yet hanging in the stars,

Shall bitterly begin his fearful date

With this night's revels; and expire the term

Of a despised life, clos'd in my breast

By some vile forfeit of untimely death.

But he that hath the steerage of my course

Direct my suit. On, lusty gentlemen!

BENVOLIO.

Strike, drum.

[Exeunt.]

SCENE V. A Hall in Capulet's House.

Musicians waiting. Enter Servants.

FIRST SERVANT.

Where's Potpan, that he helps not to take away?

He shift a trencher! He scrape a trencher!

SECOND SERVANT.

When good manners shall lie all in one or two men's hands, and they unwash'd too, 'tis a foul thing.

FIRST SERVANT.

Away with the join-stools, remove the court-cupboard, look to the plate. Good thou, save me a piece of marchpane; and as thou loves me, let the porter let in Susan Grindstone and Nell. Antony and Potpan!

SECOND SERVANT.

Ay, boy, ready.

FIRST SERVANT.

You are looked for and called for, asked for and sought for, in the great chamber.

SECOND SERVANT.

We cannot be here and there too. Cheerly, boys. Be brisk awhile, and the longer liver take all.

[Exeunt.]

Enter Capulet, &c. with the Guests and Gentlewomen to the Maskers.

CAPULET.

Welcome, gentlemen, ladies that have their toes

Unplagu'd with corns will have a bout with you.

Ah my mistresses, which of you all

Will now deny to dance? She that makes dainty,

She I'll swear hath corns. Am I come near ye now?

Welcome, gentlemen! I have seen the day

That I have worn a visor, and could tell

A whispering tale in a fair lady's ear,

Such as would please; 'tis gone, 'tis gone, 'tis gone,

You are welcome, gentlemen! Come, musicians, play.

A hall, a hall, give room! And foot it, girls.

       [Music plays, and they dance.]

More light, you knaves; and turn the tables up,

And quench the fire, the room is grown too hot.

Ah sirrah, this unlook'd-for sport comes well.

Nay sit, nay sit, good cousin Capulet,

For you and I are past our dancing days;

How long is't now since last yourself and I

Were in a mask?

CAPULET'S COUSIN.

By'r Lady, thirty years.

CAPULET.

What, man, 'tis not so much, 'tis not so much:

'Tis since the nuptial of Lucentio,

Come Pentecost as quickly as it will,

Some five and twenty years; and then we mask'd.

CAPULET'S COUSIN.

'Tis more, 'tis more, his son is elder, sir;

His son is thirty.

CAPULET.

Will you tell me that?

His son was but a ward two years ago.

ROMEO.

What lady is that, which doth enrich the hand

Of yonder knight?

SERVANT.

I know not, sir.

ROMEO.

O, she doth teach the torches to burn bright!

It seems she hangs upon the cheek of night

As a rich jewel in an Ethiop's ear;

Beauty too rich for use, for earth too dear!

So shows a snowy dove trooping with crows

As yonder lady o'er her fellows shows.

The measure done, I'll watch her place of stand,

And touching hers, make blessed my rude hand.

Did my heart love till now? Forswear it, sight!

For I ne'er saw true beauty till this night.

TYBALT.

This by his voice, should be a Montague.

Fetch me my rapier, boy. What, dares the slave

Come hither, cover'd with an antic face,

To fleer and scorn at our solemnity?

Now by the stock and honour of my kin,

To strike him dead I hold it not a sin.

CAPULET.

Why how now, kinsman!

Wherefore storm you so?

TYBALT.

Uncle, this is a Montague, our foe;

A villain that is hither come in spite,

To scorn at our solemnity this night.

CAPULET.

Young Romeo, is it?

TYBALT.

'Tis he, that villain Romeo.

CAPULET.

Content thee, gentle coz, let him alone,

A bears him like a portly gentleman;

And, to say truth, Verona brags of him

To be a virtuous and well-govern'd youth.

I would not for the wealth of all the town

Here in my house do him disparagement.

Therefore be patient, take no note of him,

It is my will; the which if thou respect,

Show a fair presence and put off these frowns,

An ill-beseeming semblance for a feast.

TYBALT.

It fits when such a villain is a guest:

I'll not endure him.

CAPULET.

He shall be endur'd.

What, goodman boy! I say he shall, go to;

Am I the master here, or you? Go to.

You'll not endure him! God shall mend my soul,

You'll make a mutiny among my guests!

You will set cock-a-hoop, you'll be the man!

TYBALT.

Why, uncle, 'tis a shame.

CAPULET.

Go to, go to!

You are a saucy boy. Is't so, indeed?

This trick may chance to scathe you, I know what.

You must contrary me! Marry, 'tis time.

Well said, my hearts!—You are a princox; go:

Be quiet, or—More light, more light!—For shame!

I'll make you quiet. What, cheerly, my hearts.

TYBALT.

Patience perforce with wilful choler meeting

Makes my flesh tremble in their different greeting.

I will withdraw: but this intrusion shall,

Now seeming sweet, convert to bitter gall.

[Exit.]

ROMEO.

[To Juliet.] If I profane with my unworthiest hand

This holy shrine, the gentle sin is this,

My lips, two blushing pilgrims, ready stand

To smooth that rough touch with a tender kiss.

JULIET.

Good pilgrim, you do wrong your hand too much,

Which mannerly devotion shows in this;

For saints have hands that pilgrims' hands do touch,

And palm to palm is holy palmers' kiss.

ROMEO.

Have not saints lips, and holy palmers too?

JULIET.

Ay, pilgrim, lips that they must use in prayer.

ROMEO.

O, then, dear saint, let lips do what hands do:

They pray, grant thou, lest faith turn to despair.

JULIET.

Saints do not move, though grant for prayers' sake.

ROMEO.

Then move not while my prayer's effect I take.

Thus from my lips, by thine my sin is purg'd.

[Kissing her.]

JULIET.

Then have my lips the sin that they have took.

ROMEO.

Sin from my lips? O trespass sweetly urg'd!

Give me my sin again.

JULIET.

You kiss by the book.

NURSE.

Madam, your mother craves a word with you.

ROMEO.

What is her mother?

NURSE.

Marry, bachelor,

Her mother is the lady of the house,

And a good lady, and a wise and virtuous.

I nurs'd her daughter that you talk'd withal.

I tell you, he that can lay hold of her

Shall have the chinks.

ROMEO.

Is she a Capulet?

O dear account! My life is my foe's debt.

BENVOLIO.

Away, be gone; the sport is at the best.

ROMEO.

Ay, so I fear; the more is my unrest.

CAPULET.

Nay, gentlemen, prepare not to be gone,

We have a trifling foolish banquet towards.

Is it e'en so? Why then, I thank you all;

I thank you, honest gentlemen; good night.

More torches here! Come on then, let's to bed.

Ah, sirrah, by my fay, it waxes late,

I'll to my rest.

[Exeunt all but Juliet and Nurse.]

JULIET.

Come hither, Nurse. What is yond gentleman?

NURSE.

The son and heir of old Tiberio.

JULIET.

What's he that now is going out of door?

NURSE.

Marry, that I think be young Petruchio.

JULIET.

What's he that follows here, that would not dance?

NURSE.

I know not.

JULIET.

Go ask his name. If he be married,

My grave is like to be my wedding bed.

NURSE.

His name is Romeo, and a Montague,

The only son of your great enemy.

JULIET.

My only love sprung from my only hate!

Too early seen unknown, and known too late!

Prodigious birth of love it is to me,

That I must love a loathed enemy.

NURSE.

What's this? What's this?

JULIET.

A rhyme I learn'd even now

Of one I danc'd withal.

[One calls within, 'Juliet'.]

NURSE.

Anon, anon!

Come let's away, the strangers all are gone.

[Exeunt.]

ACT II

CHORUS.

Now old desire doth in his deathbed lie,

And young affection gapes to be his heir;

That fair for which love groan'd for and would die,

With tender Juliet match'd, is now not fair.

Now Romeo is belov'd, and loves again,

Alike bewitched by the charm of looks;

But to his foe suppos'd he must complain,

And she steal love's sweet bait from fearful hooks:

Being held a foe, he may not have access

To breathe such vows as lovers use to swear;

And she as much in love, her means much less

To meet her new beloved anywhere.

But passion lends them power, time means, to meet,

Tempering extremities with extreme sweet.

[Exit.]

SCENE I. An open place adjoining Capulet's Garden.

Enter Romeo.

ROMEO.

Can I go forward when my heart is here?

Turn back, dull earth, and find thy centre out.

[He climbs the wall and leaps down within it.]

Enter Benvolio and Mercutio.

BENVOLIO.

Romeo! My cousin Romeo! Romeo!

MERCUTIO.

He is wise,

And on my life hath stol'n him home to bed.

BENVOLIO.

He ran this way, and leap'd this orchard wall:

Call, good Mercutio.

MERCUTIO.

Nay, I'll conjure too.

Romeo! Humours! Madman! Passion! Lover!

Appear thou in the likeness of a sigh,

Speak but one rhyme, and I am satisfied;

Cry but 'Ah me!' Pronounce but Love and dove;

Speak to my gossip Venus one fair word,

One nickname for her purblind son and heir,

Young Abraham Cupid, he that shot so trim

When King Cophetua lov'd the beggar-maid.

He heareth not, he stirreth not, he moveth not;

The ape is dead, and I must conjure him.

I conjure thee by Rosaline's bright eyes,

By her high forehead and her scarlet lip,

By her fine foot, straight leg, and quivering thigh,

And the demesnes that there adjacent lie,

That in thy likeness thou appear to us.

BENVOLIO.

An if he hear thee, thou wilt anger him.

MERCUTIO.

This cannot anger him. 'Twould anger him

To raise a spirit in his mistress' circle,

Of some strange nature, letting it there stand

Till she had laid it, and conjur'd it down;

That were some spite. My invocation

Is fair and honest, and, in his mistress' name,

I conjure only but to raise up him.

BENVOLIO.

Come, he hath hid himself among these trees

To be consorted with the humorous night.

Blind is his love, and best befits the dark.

MERCUTIO.

If love be blind, love cannot hit the mark.

Now will he sit under a medlar tree,

And wish his mistress were that kind of fruit

As maids call medlars when they laugh alone.

O Romeo, that she were, O that she were

An open-arse and thou a poperin pear!

Romeo, good night. I'll to my truckle-bed.

This field-bed is too cold for me to sleep.

Come, shall we go?

BENVOLIO.

Go then; for 'tis in vain

To seek him here that means not to be found.

[Exeunt.]

SCENE II. Capulet's Garden.

Enter Romeo.

ROMEO.

He jests at scars that never felt a wound.

Juliet appears above at a window.

But soft, what light through yonder window breaks?

It is the east, and Juliet is the sun!

Arise fair sun and kill the envious moon,

Who is already sick and pale with grief,

That thou her maid art far more fair than she.

Be not her maid since she is envious;

Her vestal livery is but sick and green,

And none but fools do wear it; cast it off.

It is my lady, O it is my love!

O, that she knew she were!

She speaks, yet she says nothing. What of that?

Her eye discourses, I will answer it.

I am too bold, 'tis not to me she speaks.

Two of the fairest stars in all the heaven,

Having some business, do entreat her eyes

To twinkle in their spheres till they return.

What if her eyes were there, they in her head?

The brightness of her cheek would shame those stars,

As daylight doth a lamp; her eyes in heaven

Would through the airy region stream so bright

That birds would sing and think it were not night.

See how she leans her cheek upon her hand.

O that I were a glove upon that hand,

That I might touch that cheek.

JULIET.

Ay me.

ROMEO.

She speaks.

O speak again bright angel, for thou art

As glorious to this night, being o'er my head,

As is a winged messenger of heaven

Unto the white-upturned wondering eyes

Of mortals that fall back to gaze on him

When he bestrides the lazy-puffing clouds

And sails upon the bosom of the air.

JULIET.

O Romeo, Romeo, wherefore art thou Romeo?

Deny thy father and refuse thy name.

Or if thou wilt not, be but sworn my love,

And I'll no longer be a Capulet.

ROMEO.

[Aside.] Shall I hear more, or shall I speak at this?

JULIET.

'Tis but thy name that is my enemy;

Thou art thyself, though not a Montague.

What's Montague? It is nor hand nor foot,

Nor arm, nor face, nor any other part

Belonging to a man. O be some other name.

What's in a name? That which we call a rose

By any other name would smell as sweet;

So Romeo would, were he not Romeo call'd,

Retain that dear perfection which he owes

Without that title. Romeo, doff thy name,

And for thy name, which is no part of thee,

Take all myself.

ROMEO.

I take thee at thy word.

Call me but love, and I'll be new baptis'd;

Henceforth I never will be Romeo.

JULIET.

What man art thou that, thus bescreen'd in night

So stumblest on my counsel?

ROMEO.

By a name

I know not how to tell thee who I am:

My name, dear saint, is hateful to myself,

Because it is an enemy to thee.

Had I it written, I would tear the word.

JULIET.

My ears have yet not drunk a hundred words

Of thy tongue's utterance, yet I know the sound.

Art thou not Romeo, and a Montague?

ROMEO.

Neither, fair maid, if either thee dislike.

JULIET.

How cam'st thou hither, tell me, and wherefore?

The orchard walls are high and hard to climb,

And the place death, considering who thou art,

If any of my kinsmen find thee here.

ROMEO.

With love's light wings did I o'erperch these walls,

For stony limits cannot hold love out,

And what love can do, that dares love attempt:

Therefore thy kinsmen are no stop to me.

JULIET.

If they do see thee, they will murder thee.

ROMEO.

Alack, there lies more peril in thine eye

Than twenty of their swords. Look thou but sweet,

And I am proof against their enmity.

JULIET.

I would not for the world they saw thee here.

ROMEO.

I have night's cloak to hide me from their eyes,

And but thou love me, let them find me here.

My life were better ended by their hate

Than death prorogued, wanting of thy love.

JULIET.

By whose direction found'st thou out this place?

ROMEO.

By love, that first did prompt me to enquire;

He lent me counsel, and I lent him eyes.

I am no pilot; yet wert thou as far

As that vast shore wash'd with the farthest sea,

I should adventure for such merchandise.

JULIET.

Thou knowest the mask of night is on my face,

Else would a maiden blush bepaint my cheek

For that which thou hast heard me speak tonight.

Fain would I dwell on form, fain, fain deny

What I have spoke; but farewell compliment.

Dost thou love me? I know thou wilt say Ay,

And I will take thy word. Yet, if thou swear'st,

Thou mayst prove false. At lovers' perjuries,

They say Jove laughs. O gentle Romeo,

If thou dost love, pronounce it faithfully.

Or if thou thinkest I am too quickly won,

I'll frown and be perverse, and say thee nay,

So thou wilt woo. But else, not for the world.

In truth, fair Montague, I am too fond;

And therefore thou mayst think my 'haviour light:

But trust me, gentleman, I'll prove more true

Than those that have more cunning to be strange.

I should have been more strange, I must confess,

But that thou overheard'st, ere I was 'ware,

My true-love passion; therefore pardon me,

And not impute this yielding to light love,

Which the dark night hath so discovered.

ROMEO.

Lady, by yonder blessed moon I vow,

That tips with silver all these fruit-tree tops,—

JULIET.

O swear not by the moon, th'inconstant moon,

That monthly changes in her circled orb,

Lest that thy love prove likewise variable.

ROMEO.

What shall I swear by?

JULIET.

Do not swear at all.

Or if thou wilt, swear by thy gracious self,

Which is the god of my idolatry,

And I'll believe thee.

ROMEO.

If my heart's dear love,—

JULIET.

Well, do not swear. Although I joy in thee,

I have no joy of this contract tonight;

It is too rash, too unadvis'd, too sudden,

Too like the lightning, which doth cease to be

Ere one can say It lightens. Sweet, good night.

This bud of love, by summer's ripening breath,

May prove a beauteous flower when next we meet.

Good night, good night. As sweet repose and rest

Come to thy heart as that within my breast.

ROMEO.

O wilt thou leave me so unsatisfied?

JULIET.

What satisfaction canst thou have tonight?

ROMEO.

Th'exchange of thy love's faithful vow for mine.

JULIET.

I gave thee mine before thou didst request it;

And yet I would it were to give again.

ROMEO.

Would'st thou withdraw it? For what purpose, love?

JULIET.

But to be frank and give it thee again.

And yet I wish but for the thing I have;

My bounty is as boundless as the sea,

My love as deep; the more I give to thee,

The more I have, for both are infinite.

I hear some noise within. Dear love, adieu.

[Nurse calls within.]

Anon, good Nurse!—Sweet Montague be true.

Stay but a little, I will come again.

[Exit.]

ROMEO.

O blessed, blessed night. I am afeard,

Being in night, all this is but a dream,

Too flattering sweet to be substantial.

Enter Juliet above.

JULIET.

Three words, dear Romeo, and good night indeed.

If that thy bent of love be honourable,

Thy purpose marriage, send me word tomorrow,

By one that I'll procure to come to thee,

Where and what time thou wilt perform the rite,

And all my fortunes at thy foot I'll lay

And follow thee my lord throughout the world.

NURSE.

[Within.] Madam.

JULIET.

I come, anon.— But if thou meanest not well,

I do beseech thee,—

NURSE.

[Within.] Madam.

JULIET.

By and by I come—

To cease thy strife and leave me to my grief.

Tomorrow will I send.

ROMEO.

So thrive my soul,—

JULIET.

A thousand times good night.

[Exit.]

ROMEO.

A thousand times the worse, to want thy light.

Love goes toward love as schoolboys from their books,

But love from love, towards school with heavy looks.

[Retiring slowly.]

Re-enter Juliet, above.

JULIET.

Hist! Romeo, hist! O for a falconer's voice

To lure this tassel-gentle back again.

Bondage is hoarse and may not speak aloud,

Else would I tear the cave where Echo lies,

And make her airy tongue more hoarse than mine

With repetition of my Romeo's name.

ROMEO.

It is my soul that calls upon my name.

How silver-sweet sound lovers' tongues by night,

Like softest music to attending ears.

JULIET.

Romeo.

ROMEO.

My nyas?

JULIET.

221

What o'clock tomorrow

Shall I send to thee?

ROMEO.

By the hour of nine.

JULIET.

I will not fail. 'Tis twenty years till then.

I have forgot why I did call thee back.

ROMEO.

Let me stand here till thou remember it.

JULIET.

I shall forget, to have thee still stand there,

Remembering how I love thy company.

ROMEO.

And I'll still stay, to have thee still forget,

Forgetting any other home but this.

JULIET.

'Tis almost morning; I would have thee gone,

And yet no farther than a wanton's bird,

That lets it hop a little from her hand,

Like a poor prisoner in his twisted gyves,

And with a silk thread plucks it back again,

So loving-jealous of his liberty.

ROMEO.

I would I were thy bird.

JULIET.

Sweet, so would I:

Yet I should kill thee with much cherishing.

Good night, good night. Parting is such sweet sorrow

That I shall say good night till it be morrow.

[Exit.]

ROMEO.

Sleep dwell upon thine eyes, peace in thy breast.

Would I were sleep and peace, so sweet to rest.

The grey-ey'd morn smiles on the frowning night,

Chequering the eastern clouds with streaks of light;

And darkness fleckled like a drunkard reels

From forth day's pathway, made by Titan's wheels

Hence will I to my ghostly Sire's cell,

His help to crave and my dear hap to tell.

[Exit.]

SCENE III. Friar Lawrence's Cell.

Enter Friar Lawrence with a basket.

FRIAR LAWRENCE.

Now, ere the sun advance his burning eye,

The day to cheer, and night's dank dew to dry,

I must upfill this osier cage of ours

With baleful weeds and precious-juiced flowers.

The earth that's nature's mother, is her tomb;

What is her burying grave, that is her womb:

And from her womb children of divers kind

We sucking on her natural bosom find.

Many for many virtues excellent,

None but for some, and yet all different.

O, mickle is the powerful grace that lies

In plants, herbs, stones, and their true qualities.

For naught so vile that on the earth doth live

But to the earth some special good doth give;

Nor aught so good but, strain'd from that fair use,

Revolts from true birth, stumbling on abuse.

Virtue itself turns vice being misapplied,

And vice sometime's by action dignified.

Enter Romeo.

Within the infant rind of this weak flower

Poison hath residence, and medicine power:

For this, being smelt, with that part cheers each part;

Being tasted, slays all senses with the heart.

Two such opposed kings encamp them still

In man as well as herbs,—grace and rude will;

And where the worser is predominant,

Full soon the canker death eats up that plant.

ROMEO.

Good morrow, father.

FRIAR LAWRENCE.

Benedicite!

What early tongue so sweet saluteth me?

Young son, it argues a distemper'd head

So soon to bid good morrow to thy bed.

Care keeps his watch in every old man's eye,

And where care lodges sleep will never lie;

But where unbruised youth with unstuff'd brain

Doth couch his limbs, there golden sleep doth reign.

Therefore thy earliness doth me assure

Thou art uprous'd with some distemperature;

Or if not so, then here I hit it right,

Our Romeo hath not been in bed tonight.

ROMEO.

That last is true; the sweeter rest was mine.

FRIAR LAWRENCE.

God pardon sin. Wast thou with Rosaline?

ROMEO.

With Rosaline, my ghostly father? No.

I have forgot that name, and that name's woe.

FRIAR LAWRENCE.

That's my good son. But where hast thou been then?

ROMEO.

I'll tell thee ere thou ask it me again.

I have been feasting with mine enemy,

Where on a sudden one hath wounded me

That's by me wounded. Both our remedies

Within thy help and holy physic lies.

I bear no hatred, blessed man; for lo,

My intercession likewise steads my foe.

FRIAR LAWRENCE.

Be plain, good son, and homely in thy drift;

Riddling confession finds but riddling shrift.

ROMEO.

Then plainly know my heart's dear love is set

On the fair daughter of rich Capulet.

As mine on hers, so hers is set on mine;

And all combin'd, save what thou must combine

By holy marriage. When, and where, and how

We met, we woo'd, and made exchange of vow,

I'll tell thee as we pass; but this I pray,

That thou consent to marry us today.

FRIAR LAWRENCE.

Holy Saint Francis! What a change is here!

Is Rosaline, that thou didst love so dear,

So soon forsaken? Young men's love then lies

Not truly in their hearts, but in their eyes.

Jesu Maria, what a deal of brine

Hath wash'd thy sallow cheeks for Rosaline!

How much salt water thrown away in waste,

To season love, that of it doth not taste.

The sun not yet thy sighs from heaven clears,

Thy old groans yet ring in mine ancient ears.

Lo here upon thy cheek the stain doth sit

Of an old tear that is not wash'd off yet.

If ere thou wast thyself, and these woes thine,

Thou and these woes were all for Rosaline,

And art thou chang'd? Pronounce this sentence then,

Women may fall, when there's no strength in men.

ROMEO.

Thou chidd'st me oft for loving Rosaline.

FRIAR LAWRENCE.

For doting, not for loving, pupil mine.

ROMEO.

And bad'st me bury love.

FRIAR LAWRENCE.

Not in a grave

To lay one in, another out to have.

ROMEO.

I pray thee chide me not, her I love now

Doth grace for grace and love for love allow.

The other did not so.

FRIAR LAWRENCE.

O, she knew well

Thy love did read by rote, that could not spell.

But come young waverer, come go with me,

In one respect I'll thy assistant be;

For this alliance may so happy prove,

To turn your households' rancour to pure love.

ROMEO.

O let us hence; I stand on sudden haste.

FRIAR LAWRENCE.

Wisely and slow; they stumble that run fast.

[Exeunt.]

SCENE IV. A Street.

Enter Benvolio and Mercutio.

MERCUTIO.

Where the devil should this Romeo be? Came he not home tonight?

BENVOLIO.

Not to his father's; I spoke with his man.

MERCUTIO.

Why, that same pale hard-hearted wench, that Rosaline, torments him so that he will sure run mad.

BENVOLIO.

Tybalt, the kinsman to old Capulet, hath sent a letter to his father's house.

MERCUTIO.

A challenge, on my life.

BENVOLIO.

Romeo will answer it.

MERCUTIO.

Any man that can write may answer a letter.

BENVOLIO.

Nay, he will answer the letter's master, how he dares, being dared.

MERCUTIO.

Alas poor Romeo, he is already dead, stabbed with a white wench's black eye; run through the ear with a love song, the very pin of his heart cleft with the blind bow-boy's butt-shaft. And is he a man to encounter Tybalt?

BENVOLIO.

Why, what is Tybalt?

MERCUTIO.

More than Prince of cats. O, he's the courageous captain of compliments. He fights as you sing prick-song, keeps time, distance, and proportion. He rests his minim rest, one, two, and the third in your bosom: the very butcher of a silk button, a duellist, a duellist; a gentleman of the very first house, of the first and second cause. Ah, the immortal passado, the punto reverso, the hay.

BENVOLIO.

The what?

MERCUTIO.

The pox of such antic lisping, affecting phantasies; these new tuners of accent. By Jesu, a very good blade, a very tall man, a very good whore. Why, is not this a lamentable thing, grandsire, that we should be thus afflicted with these strange flies, these fashion-mongers, these pardon-me's, who stand so much on the new form that they cannot sit at ease on the old bench? O their bones, their bones!

Enter Romeo.

BENVOLIO.

Here comes Romeo, here comes Romeo!

MERCUTIO.

Without his roe, like a dried herring. O flesh, flesh, how art thou fishified! Now is he for the numbers that Petrarch flowed in. Laura, to his lady, was but a kitchen wench,—marry, she had a better love to berhyme her: Dido a dowdy; Cleopatra a gypsy; Helen and Hero hildings and harlots; Thisbe a grey eye or so, but not to the purpose. Signior Romeo, bonjour!

There's a French salutation to your French slop. You gave us the counterfeit fairly last night.

ROMEO.

Good morrow to you both. What counterfeit did I give you?

MERCUTIO.

The slip sir, the slip; can you not conceive?

ROMEO.

Pardon, good Mercutio, my business was great, and in such a case as mine a man may strain courtesy.

MERCUTIO.

That's as much as to say, such a case as yours constrains a man to bow in the hams.

ROMEO.

Meaning, to curtsy.

MERCUTIO.

Thou hast most kindly hit it.

ROMEO.

A most courteous exposition.

MERCUTIO.

Nay, I am the very pink of courtesy.

ROMEO.

Pink for flower.

MERCUTIO.

Right.

ROMEO.

Why, then is my pump well flowered.

MERCUTIO.

Sure wit, follow me this jest now, till thou hast worn out thy pump, that when the single sole of it is worn, the jest may remain after the wearing, solely singular.

ROMEO.

O single-soled jest, solely singular for the singleness!

MERCUTIO.

Come between us, good Benvolio; my wits faint.

ROMEO.

Swits and spurs, swits and spurs; or I'll cry a match.

MERCUTIO.

Nay, if thy wits run the wild-goose chase, I am done. For thou hast more of the wild-goose in one of thy wits, than I am sure, I have in my whole five. Was I with you there for the goose?

ROMEO.

Thou wast never with me for anything, when thou wast not there for the goose.

MERCUTIO.

I will bite thee by the ear for that jest.

ROMEO.

Nay, good goose, bite not.

MERCUTIO.

Thy wit is a very bitter sweeting, it is a most sharp sauce.

ROMEO.

And is it not then well served in to a sweet goose?

MERCUTIO.

O here's a wit of cheveril, that stretches from an inch narrow to an ell broad.

ROMEO.

I stretch it out for that word broad, which added to the goose, proves thee far and wide a broad goose.

MERCUTIO.

Why, is not this better now than groaning for love? Now art thou sociable, now art thou Romeo; not art thou what thou art, by art as well as by nature. For this drivelling love is like a great natural, that runs lolling up and down to hide his bauble in a hole.

BENVOLIO.

Stop there, stop there.

MERCUTIO.

Thou desirest me to stop in my tale against the hair.

BENVOLIO.

Thou wouldst else have made thy tale large.

MERCUTIO.

O, thou art deceived; I would have made it short, for I was come to the whole depth of my tale, and meant indeed to occupy the argument no longer.

Enter Nurse and Peter.

ROMEO.

Here's goodly gear!

A sail, a sail!

MERCUTIO.

Two, two; a shirt and a smock.

NURSE.

Peter!

PETER.

Anon.

NURSE.

My fan, Peter.

MERCUTIO.

Good Peter, to hide her face; for her fan's the fairer face.

NURSE.

God ye good morrow, gentlemen.

MERCUTIO.

God ye good-den, fair gentlewoman.

NURSE.

Is it good-den?

MERCUTIO.

'Tis no less, I tell ye; for the bawdy hand of the dial is now upon the prick of noon.

NURSE.

Out upon you! What a man are you?

ROMEO.

One, gentlewoman, that God hath made for himself to mar.

NURSE.

By my troth, it is well said; for himself to mar, quoth a? Gentlemen, can any of you tell me where I may find the young Romeo?

ROMEO.

I can tell you: but young Romeo will be older when you have found him than he was when you sought him. I am the youngest of that name, for fault of a worse.

NURSE.

You say well.

MERCUTIO.

Yea, is the worst well? Very well took, i'faith; wisely, wisely.

NURSE.

If you be he, sir, I desire some confidence with you.

BENVOLIO.

She will endite him to some supper.

MERCUTIO.

A bawd, a bawd, a bawd! So ho!

ROMEO.

What hast thou found?

MERCUTIO.

No hare, sir; unless a hare, sir, in a lenten pie, that is something stale and hoar ere it be spent.

[Sings.]

An old hare hoar,

And an old hare hoar,

Is very good meat in Lent;

But a hare that is hoar

Is too much for a score

When it hoars ere it be spent.

Romeo, will you come to your father's? We'll to dinner thither.

ROMEO.

I will follow you.

MERCUTIO.

Farewell, ancient lady; farewell, lady, lady, lady.

[Exeunt Mercutio and Benvolio.]

NURSE.

I pray you, sir, what saucy merchant was this that was so full of his ropery?

ROMEO.

A gentleman, Nurse, that loves to hear himself talk, and will speak more in a minute than he will stand to in a month.

NURSE.

And a speak anything against me, I'll take him down, and a were lustier than he is, and twenty such Jacks. And if I cannot, I'll find those that shall. Scurvy knave! I am none of his flirt-gills; I am none of his skains-mates.— And thou must stand by too and suffer every knave to use me at his pleasure!

PETER.

I saw no man use you at his pleasure; if I had, my weapon should quickly have been out. I warrant you, I dare draw as soon as another man, if I see occasion in a good quarrel, and the law on my side.

NURSE.

Now, afore God, I am so vexed that every part about me quivers. Scurvy knave. Pray you, sir, a word: and as I told you, my young lady bid me enquire you out; what she bade me say, I will keep to myself. But first let me tell ye, if ye should lead her in a fool's paradise, as they say, it were a very gross kind of behaviour, as they say; for the gentlewoman is young. And therefore, if you should deal double with her, truly it were an ill thing to be offered to any gentlewoman, and very weak dealing.

ROMEO.

Nurse, commend me to thy lady and mistress. I protest unto thee,—

NURSE.

Good heart, and i'faith I will tell her as much. Lord, Lord, she will be a joyful woman.

ROMEO.

What wilt thou tell her, Nurse? Thou dost not mark me.

NURSE.

I will tell her, sir, that you do protest, which, as I take it, is a gentlemanlike offer.

ROMEO.

Bid her devise

Some means to come to shrift this afternoon,

And there she shall at Friar Lawrence' cell

Be shriv'd and married. Here is for thy pains.

NURSE.

No truly, sir; not a penny.

ROMEO.

Go to; I say you shall.

NURSE.

This afternoon, sir? Well, she shall be there.

ROMEO.

And stay, good Nurse, behind the abbey wall.

Within this hour my man shall be with thee,

And bring thee cords made like a tackled stair,

Which to the high topgallant of my joy

Must be my convoy in the secret night.

Farewell, be trusty, and I'll quit thy pains;

Farewell; commend me to thy mistress.

NURSE.

Now God in heaven bless thee. Hark you, sir.

ROMEO.

What say'st thou, my dear Nurse?

NURSE.

Is your man secret? Did you ne'er hear say,

Two may keep counsel, putting one away?

ROMEO.

I warrant thee my man's as true as steel.

NURSE.

Well, sir, my mistress is the sweetest lady. Lord, Lord! When 'twas a little prating thing,—O, there is a nobleman in town, one Paris, that would fain lay knife aboard; but she, good soul, had as lief see a toad, a very toad, as see him. I anger her sometimes, and tell her that Paris is the properer man, but I'll warrant you, when I say so, she looks as pale as any clout in the versal world. Doth not rosemary and Romeo begin both with a letter?

ROMEO.

Ay, Nurse; what of that? Both with an R.

NURSE.

Ah, mocker! That's the dog's name. R is for the—no, I know it begins with some other letter, and she hath the prettiest sententious of it, of you and rosemary, that it would do you good to hear it.

ROMEO.

Commend me to thy lady.

NURSE.

Ay, a thousand times. Peter!

[Exit Romeo.]

PETER.

Anon.

NURSE.

Before and apace.

[Exeunt.]

SCENE V. Capulet's Garden.

Enter Juliet.

JULIET.

The clock struck nine when I did send the Nurse,

In half an hour she promised to return.

Perchance she cannot meet him. That's not so.

O, she is lame. Love's heralds should be thoughts,

Which ten times faster glides than the sun's beams,

Driving back shadows over lowering hills:

Therefore do nimble-pinion'd doves draw love,

And therefore hath the wind-swift Cupid wings.

Now is the sun upon the highmost hill

Of this day's journey, and from nine till twelve

Is three long hours, yet she is not come.

Had she affections and warm youthful blood,

She'd be as swift in motion as a ball;

My words would bandy her to my sweet love,

And his to me.

But old folks, many feign as they were dead;

Unwieldy, slow, heavy and pale as lead.

Enter Nurse and Peter.

O God, she comes. O honey Nurse, what news?

Hast thou met with him? Send thy man away.

NURSE.

Peter, stay at the gate.

[Exit Peter.]

JULIET.

Now, good sweet Nurse,—O Lord, why look'st thou sad?

Though news be sad, yet tell them merrily;

If good, thou sham'st the music of sweet news

By playing it to me with so sour a face.

NURSE.

I am aweary, give me leave awhile;

Fie, how my bones ache! What a jaunt have I had!

JULIET.

I would thou hadst my bones, and I thy news:

Nay come, I pray thee speak; good, good Nurse, speak.

NURSE.

Jesu, what haste? Can you not stay a while? Do you not see that I am out of breath?

JULIET.

How art thou out of breath, when thou hast breath

To say to me that thou art out of breath?

The excuse that thou dost make in this delay

Is longer than the tale thou dost excuse.

Is thy news good or bad? Answer to that;

Say either, and I'll stay the circumstance.

Let me be satisfied, is't good or bad?

NURSE.

Well, you have made a simple choice; you know not how to choose a man. Romeo? No, not he. Though his face be better than any man's, yet his leg excels all men's, and for a hand and a foot, and a body, though they be not to be talked on, yet they are past compare. He is not the flower of courtesy, but I'll warrant him as gentle as a lamb. Go thy ways, wench, serve God. What, have you dined at home?

JULIET.

No, no. But all this did I know before.

What says he of our marriage? What of that?

NURSE.

Lord, how my head aches! What a head have I!

It beats as it would fall in twenty pieces.

My back o' t'other side,—O my back, my back!

Beshrew your heart for sending me about

To catch my death with jauncing up and down.

JULIET.

I'faith, I am sorry that thou art not well.

Sweet, sweet, sweet Nurse, tell me, what says my love?

NURSE.

Your love says like an honest gentleman,

And a courteous, and a kind, and a handsome,

And I warrant a virtuous,—Where is your mother?

JULIET.

Where is my mother? Why, she is within.

Where should she be? How oddly thou repliest.

'Your love says, like an honest gentleman,

'Where is your mother?'

NURSE.

O God's lady dear,

Are you so hot? Marry, come up, I trow.

Is this the poultice for my aching bones?

Henceforward do your messages yourself.

JULIET.

Here's such a coil. Come, what says Romeo?

NURSE.

Have you got leave to go to shrift today?

JULIET.

I have.

NURSE.

Then hie you hence to Friar Lawrence' cell;

There stays a husband to make you a wife.

Now comes the wanton blood up in your cheeks,

They'll be in scarlet straight at any news.

Hie you to church. I must another way,

To fetch a ladder by the which your love

Must climb a bird's nest soon when it is dark.

I am the drudge, and toil in your delight;

But you shall bear the burden soon at night.

Go. I'll to dinner; hie you to the cell.

JULIET.

Hie to high fortune! Honest Nurse, farewell.

[Exeunt.]

SCENE VI. Friar Lawrence's Cell.

Enter Friar Lawrence and Romeo.

FRIAR LAWRENCE.

So smile the heavens upon this holy act

That after-hours with sorrow chide us not.

ROMEO.

Amen, amen, but come what sorrow can,

It cannot countervail the exchange of joy

That one short minute gives me in her sight.

Do thou but close our hands with holy words,

Then love-devouring death do what he dare,

It is enough I may but call her mine.

FRIAR LAWRENCE.

These violent delights have violent ends,

And in their triumph die; like fire and powder,

Which as they kiss consume. The sweetest honey

Is loathsome in his own deliciousness,

And in the taste confounds the appetite.

Therefore love moderately: long love doth so;

Too swift arrives as tardy as too slow.

Enter Juliet.

Here comes the lady. O, so light a foot

Will ne'er wear out the everlasting flint.

A lover may bestride the gossamers

That idles in the wanton summer air

And yet not fall; so light is vanity.

JULIET.

Good even to my ghostly confessor.

FRIAR LAWRENCE.

Romeo shall thank thee, daughter, for us both.

JULIET.

As much to him, else is his thanks too much.

ROMEO.

Ah, Juliet, if the measure of thy joy

Be heap'd like mine, and that thy skill be more

To blazon it, then sweeten with thy breath

This neighbour air, and let rich music's tongue

Unfold the imagin'd happiness that both

Receive in either by this dear encounter.

JULIET.

Conceit more rich in matter than in words,

Brags of his substance, not of ornament.

They are but beggars that can count their worth;

But my true love is grown to such excess,

I cannot sum up sum of half my wealth.

FRIAR LAWRENCE.

Come, come with me, and we will make short work,

For, by your leaves, you shall not stay alone

Till holy church incorporate two in one.

[Exeunt.]

ACT III

SCENE I. A public Place.

Enter Mercutio, Benvolio, Page and Servants.

BENVOLIO.

I pray thee, good Mercutio, let's retire:

The day is hot, the Capulets abroad,

And if we meet, we shall not scape a brawl,

For now these hot days, is the mad blood stirring.

MERCUTIO.

Thou art like one of these fellows that, when he enters the confines of a tavern, claps me his sword upon the table, and says 'God send me no need of thee!' and by the operation of the second cup draws him on the drawer, when indeed there is no need.

BENVOLIO.

Am I like such a fellow?

MERCUTIO.

Come, come, thou art as hot a Jack in thy mood as any in Italy; and as soon moved to be moody, and as soon moody to be moved.

BENVOLIO.

And what to?

MERCUTIO.

Nay, an there were two such, we should have none shortly, for one would kill the other. Thou? Why, thou wilt quarrel with a man that hath a hair more or a hair less in his beard than thou hast. Thou wilt quarrel with a man for cracking nuts, having no other reason but because thou hast hazel eyes. What eye but such an eye would spy out such a quarrel? Thy head is as full of quarrels as an egg is full of meat, and yet thy head hath been beaten as addle as an egg for quarrelling. Thou hast quarrelled with a man for coughing in the street, because he hath wakened thy dog that hath lain asleep in the sun. Didst thou not fall out with a tailor for wearing his new doublet before Easter? with another for tying his new shoes with an old riband? And yet thou wilt tutor me from quarrelling!

BENVOLIO.

And I were so apt to quarrel as thou art, any man should buy the fee simple of my life for an hour and a quarter.

MERCUTIO.

The fee simple! O simple!

Enter Tybalt and others.

BENVOLIO.

By my head, here comes the Capulets.

MERCUTIO.

By my heel, I care not.

TYBALT.

Follow me close, for I will speak to them.

Gentlemen, good-den: a word with one of you.

MERCUTIO.

And but one word with one of us? Couple it with something; make it a word and a blow.

TYBALT.

You shall find me apt enough to that, sir, and you will give me occasion.

MERCUTIO.

Could you not take some occasion without giving?

TYBALT.

Mercutio, thou consortest with Romeo.

MERCUTIO.

Consort? What, dost thou make us minstrels? And thou make minstrels of us, look to hear nothing but discords. Here's my fiddlestick, here's that shall make you dance. Zounds, consort!

BENVOLIO.

We talk here in the public haunt of men.

Either withdraw unto some private place,

And reason coldly of your grievances,

Or else depart; here all eyes gaze on us.

MERCUTIO.

Men's eyes were made to look, and let them gaze.

I will not budge for no man's pleasure, I.

Enter Romeo.

TYBALT.

Well, peace be with you, sir, here comes my man.

MERCUTIO.

But I'll be hanged, sir, if he wear your livery.

Marry, go before to field, he'll be your follower;

Your worship in that sense may call him man.

TYBALT.

Romeo, the love I bear thee can afford

No better term than this: Thou art a villain.

ROMEO.

Tybalt, the reason that I have to love thee

Doth much excuse the appertaining rage

To such a greeting. Villain am I none;

Therefore farewell; I see thou know'st me not.

TYBALT.

Boy, this shall not excuse the injuries

That thou hast done me, therefore turn and draw.

ROMEO.

I do protest I never injur'd thee,

But love thee better than thou canst devise

Till thou shalt know the reason of my love.

And so good Capulet, which name I tender

As dearly as mine own, be satisfied.

MERCUTIO.

O calm, dishonourable, vile submission!

[Draws.] Alla stoccata carries it away.

Tybalt, you rat-catcher, will you walk?

TYBALT.

What wouldst thou have with me?

MERCUTIO.

Good King of Cats, nothing but one of your nine lives; that I mean to make bold withal, and, as you shall use me hereafter, dry-beat the rest of the eight. Will you pluck your sword out of his pilcher by the ears? Make haste, lest mine be about your ears ere it be out.

TYBALT.

[Drawing.] I am for you.

ROMEO.

Gentle Mercutio, put thy rapier up.

MERCUTIO.

Come, sir, your passado.

[They fight.]

ROMEO.

Draw, Benvolio; beat down their weapons.

Gentlemen, for shame, forbear this outrage,

Tybalt, Mercutio, the Prince expressly hath

Forbid this bandying in Verona streets.

Hold, Tybalt! Good Mercutio!

[Exeunt Tybalt with his Partizans.]

MERCUTIO.

I am hurt.

A plague o' both your houses. I am sped.

Is he gone, and hath nothing?

BENVOLIO.

What, art thou hurt?

MERCUTIO.

Ay, ay, a scratch, a scratch. Marry, 'tis enough.

Where is my page? Go villain, fetch a surgeon.

[Exit Page.]

ROMEO.

Courage, man; the hurt cannot be much.

MERCUTIO.

No, 'tis not so deep as a well, nor so wide as a church door, but 'tis enough, 'twill serve. Ask for me tomorrow, and you shall find me a grave man. I am peppered, I warrant, for this world. A plague o' both your houses. Zounds, a dog, a rat, a mouse, a cat, to scratch a man to death. A braggart, a rogue, a villain, that fights by the book of arithmetic!—Why the devil came you between us? I was hurt under your arm.

ROMEO.

I thought all for the best.

MERCUTIO.

Help me into some house, Benvolio,

Or I shall faint. A plague o' both your houses.

They have made worms' meat of me.

I have it, and soundly too. Your houses!

[Exeunt Mercutio and Benvolio.]

ROMEO.

This gentleman, the Prince's near ally,

My very friend, hath got his mortal hurt

In my behalf; my reputation stain'd

With Tybalt's slander,—Tybalt, that an hour

Hath been my cousin. O sweet Juliet,

Thy beauty hath made me effeminate

And in my temper soften'd valour's steel.

Re-enter Benvolio.

BENVOLIO.

O Romeo, Romeo, brave Mercutio's dead,

That gallant spirit hath aspir'd the clouds,

Which too untimely here did scorn the earth.

ROMEO.

This day's black fate on mo days doth depend;

This but begins the woe others must end.

Re-enter Tybalt.

BENVOLIO.

Here comes the furious Tybalt back again.

ROMEO.

Again in triumph, and Mercutio slain?

Away to heaven respective lenity,

And fire-ey'd fury be my conduct now!

Now, Tybalt, take the 'villain' back again

That late thou gav'st me, for Mercutio's soul

Is but a little way above our heads,

Staying for thine to keep him company.

Either thou or I, or both, must go with him.

TYBALT.

Thou wretched boy, that didst consort him here,

Shalt with him hence.

ROMEO.

This shall determine that.

[They fight; Tybalt falls.]

BENVOLIO.

Romeo, away, be gone!

The citizens are up, and Tybalt slain.

Stand not amaz'd. The Prince will doom thee death

If thou art taken. Hence, be gone, away!

ROMEO.

O, I am fortune's fool!

BENVOLIO.

Why dost thou stay?

[Exit Romeo.]

Enter Citizens.

FIRST CITIZEN.

Which way ran he that kill'd Mercutio?

Tybalt, that murderer, which way ran he?

BENVOLIO.

There lies that Tybalt.

FIRST CITIZEN.

Up, sir, go with me.

I charge thee in the Prince's name obey.

255

Enter Prince, attended; Montague, Capulet, their Wives and others.

PRINCE.

Where are the vile beginners of this fray?

BENVOLIO.

O noble Prince, I can discover all

The unlucky manage of this fatal brawl.

There lies the man, slain by young Romeo,

That slew thy kinsman, brave Mercutio.

LADY CAPULET.

Tybalt, my cousin! O my brother's child!

O Prince! O husband! O, the blood is spill'd

Of my dear kinsman! Prince, as thou art true,

For blood of ours shed blood of Montague.

O cousin, cousin.

PRINCE.

Benvolio, who began this bloody fray?

BENVOLIO.

Tybalt, here slain, whom Romeo's hand did slay;

Romeo, that spoke him fair, bid him bethink

How nice the quarrel was, and urg'd withal

Your high displeasure. All this uttered

With gentle breath, calm look, knees humbly bow'd

Could not take truce with the unruly spleen

Of Tybalt, deaf to peace, but that he tilts

With piercing steel at bold Mercutio's breast,

Who, all as hot, turns deadly point to point,

And, with a martial scorn, with one hand beats

Cold death aside, and with the other sends

It back to Tybalt, whose dexterity

Retorts it. Romeo he cries aloud,

'Hold, friends! Friends, part!' and swifter than his tongue,

His agile arm beats down their fatal points,

And 'twixt them rushes; underneath whose arm

An envious thrust from Tybalt hit the life

Of stout Mercutio, and then Tybalt fled.

But by and by comes back to Romeo,

Who had but newly entertain'd revenge,

And to't they go like lightning; for, ere I

Could draw to part them was stout Tybalt slain;

And as he fell did Romeo turn and fly.

This is the truth, or let Benvolio die.

LADY CAPULET.

He is a kinsman to the Montague.

Affection makes him false, he speaks not true.

Some twenty of them fought in this black strife,

And all those twenty could but kill one life.

I beg for justice, which thou, Prince, must give;

Romeo slew Tybalt, Romeo must not live.

PRINCE.

Romeo slew him, he slew Mercutio.

Who now the price of his dear blood doth owe?

MONTAGUE.

Not Romeo, Prince, he was Mercutio's friend;

His fault concludes but what the law should end,

The life of Tybalt.

PRINCE.

And for that offence

Immediately we do exile him hence.

I have an interest in your hate's proceeding,

My blood for your rude brawls doth lie a-bleeding.

But I'll amerce you with so strong a fine

That you shall all repent the loss of mine.

I will be deaf to pleading and excuses;

Nor tears nor prayers shall purchase out abuses.

Therefore use none. Let Romeo hence in haste,

Else, when he is found, that hour is his last.

Bear hence this body, and attend our will.

Mercy but murders, pardoning those that kill.

[Exeunt.]

SCENE II. A Room in Capulet's House.

Enter Juliet.

JULIET.

Gallop apace, you fiery-footed steeds,

Towards Phoebus' lodging. Such a waggoner

As Phaeton would whip you to the west

And bring in cloudy night immediately.

Spread thy close curtain, love-performing night,

That runaway's eyes may wink, and Romeo

Leap to these arms, untalk'd of and unseen.

Lovers can see to do their amorous rites

By their own beauties: or, if love be blind,

It best agrees with night. Come, civil night,

Thou sober-suited matron, all in black,

And learn me how to lose a winning match,

Play'd for a pair of stainless maidenhoods.

Hood my unmann'd blood, bating in my cheeks,

With thy black mantle, till strange love, grow bold,

Think true love acted simple modesty.

Come, night, come Romeo; come, thou day in night;

For thou wilt lie upon the wings of night

Whiter than new snow upon a raven's back.

Come gentle night, come loving black-brow'd night,

Give me my Romeo, and when I shall die,

Take him and cut him out in little stars,

And he will make the face of heaven so fine

That all the world will be in love with night,

And pay no worship to the garish sun.

O, I have bought the mansion of a love,

But not possess'd it; and though I am sold,

Not yet enjoy'd. So tedious is this day

As is the night before some festival

To an impatient child that hath new robes

And may not wear them. O, here comes my Nurse,

And she brings news, and every tongue that speaks

But Romeo's name speaks heavenly eloquence.

Enter Nurse, with cords.

Now, Nurse, what news? What hast thou there?

The cords that Romeo bid thee fetch?

NURSE.

Ay, ay, the cords.

[Throws them down.]

JULIET.

Ay me, what news? Why dost thou wring thy hands?

NURSE.

Ah, well-a-day, he's dead, he's dead, he's dead!

260

We are undone, lady, we are undone.

Alack the day, he's gone, he's kill'd, he's dead.

JULIET.

Can heaven be so envious?

NURSE.

Romeo can,

Though heaven cannot. O Romeo, Romeo.

Who ever would have thought it? Romeo!

JULIET.

What devil art thou, that dost torment me thus?

This torture should be roar'd in dismal hell.

Hath Romeo slain himself? Say thou but Ay,

And that bare vowel I shall poison more

Than the death-darting eye of cockatrice.

I am not I if there be such an I;

Or those eyes shut that make thee answer Ay.

If he be slain, say Ay; or if not, No.

Brief sounds determine of my weal or woe.

NURSE.

I saw the wound, I saw it with mine eyes,

God save the mark!—here on his manly breast.

A piteous corse, a bloody piteous corse;

Pale, pale as ashes, all bedaub'd in blood,

261

All in gore-blood. I swounded at the sight.

JULIET.

O, break, my heart. Poor bankrout, break at once.

To prison, eyes; ne'er look on liberty.

Vile earth to earth resign; end motion here,

And thou and Romeo press one heavy bier.

NURSE.

O Tybalt, Tybalt, the best friend I had.

O courteous Tybalt, honest gentleman!

That ever I should live to see thee dead.

JULIET.

What storm is this that blows so contrary?

Is Romeo slaughter'd and is Tybalt dead?

My dearest cousin, and my dearer lord?

Then dreadful trumpet sound the general doom,

For who is living, if those two are gone?

NURSE.

Tybalt is gone, and Romeo banished,

Romeo that kill'd him, he is banished.

JULIET.

O God! Did Romeo's hand shed Tybalt's blood?

NURSE.

It did, it did; alas the day, it did.

JULIET.

O serpent heart, hid with a flowering face!

Did ever dragon keep so fair a cave?

Beautiful tyrant, fiend angelical,

Dove-feather'd raven, wolvish-ravening lamb!

Despised substance of divinest show!

Just opposite to what thou justly seem'st,

A damned saint, an honourable villain!

O nature, what hadst thou to do in hell

When thou didst bower the spirit of a fiend

In mortal paradise of such sweet flesh?

Was ever book containing such vile matter

So fairly bound? O, that deceit should dwell

In such a gorgeous palace.

NURSE.

There's no trust,

No faith, no honesty in men. All perjur'd,

All forsworn, all naught, all dissemblers.

Ah, where's my man? Give me some aqua vitae.

These griefs, these woes, these sorrows make me old.

Shame come to Romeo.

JULIET.

Blister'd be thy tongue

For such a wish! He was not born to shame.

Upon his brow shame is asham'd to sit;

For 'tis a throne where honour may be crown'd

Sole monarch of the universal earth.

O, what a beast was I to chide at him!

NURSE.

Will you speak well of him that kill'd your cousin?

JULIET.

Shall I speak ill of him that is my husband?

Ah, poor my lord, what tongue shall smooth thy name,

When I thy three-hours' wife have mangled it?

But wherefore, villain, didst thou kill my cousin?

That villain cousin would have kill'd my husband.

Back, foolish tears, back to your native spring,

Your tributary drops belong to woe,

Which you mistaking offer up to joy.

My husband lives, that Tybalt would have slain,

And Tybalt's dead, that would have slain my husband.

All this is comfort; wherefore weep I then?

Some word there was, worser than Tybalt's death,

That murder'd me. I would forget it fain,

But O, it presses to my memory

Like damned guilty deeds to sinners' minds.

Tybalt is dead, and Romeo banished.

That 'banished,' that one word 'banished,'

Hath slain ten thousand Tybalts. Tybalt's death

Was woe enough, if it had ended there.

Or if sour woe delights in fellowship,

And needly will be rank'd with other griefs,

Why follow'd not, when she said Tybalt's dead,

Thy father or thy mother, nay or both,

Which modern lamentation might have mov'd?

But with a rear-ward following Tybalt's death,

'Romeo is banished'—to speak that word

Is father, mother, Tybalt, Romeo, Juliet,

All slain, all dead. Romeo is banished,

There is no end, no limit, measure, bound,

In that word's death, no words can that woe sound.

Where is my father and my mother, Nurse?

NURSE.

Weeping and wailing over Tybalt's corse.

Will you go to them? I will bring you thither.

JULIET.

Wash they his wounds with tears. Mine shall be spent,

When theirs are dry, for Romeo's banishment.

Take up those cords. Poor ropes, you are beguil'd,

Both you and I; for Romeo is exil'd.

He made you for a highway to my bed,

But I, a maid, die maiden-widowed.

Come cords, come Nurse, I'll to my wedding bed,

And death, not Romeo, take my maidenhead.

NURSE.

Hie to your chamber. I'll find Romeo

To comfort you. I wot well where he is.

Hark ye, your Romeo will be here at night.

I'll to him, he is hid at Lawrence' cell.

JULIET.

O find him, give this ring to my true knight,

And bid him come to take his last farewell.

[Exeunt.]

SCENE III. Friar Lawrence's cell.

Enter Friar Lawrence.

FRIAR LAWRENCE.

Romeo, come forth; come forth, thou fearful man.

Affliction is enamour'd of thy parts

And thou art wedded to calamity.

Enter Romeo.

ROMEO.

Father, what news? What is the Prince's doom?

What sorrow craves acquaintance at my hand,

That I yet know not?

FRIAR LAWRENCE.

Too familiar

Is my dear son with such sour company.

I bring thee tidings of the Prince's doom.

ROMEO.

What less than doomsday is the Prince's doom?

FRIAR LAWRENCE.

A gentler judgment vanish'd from his lips,

Not body's death, but body's banishment.

ROMEO.

Ha, banishment? Be merciful, say death;

For exile hath more terror in his look,

Much more than death. Do not say banishment.

FRIAR LAWRENCE.

Hence from Verona art thou banished.

Be patient, for the world is broad and wide.

ROMEO.

There is no world without Verona walls,

But purgatory, torture, hell itself.

Hence banished is banish'd from the world,

And world's exile is death. Then banished

Is death misterm'd. Calling death banished,

Thou cutt'st my head off with a golden axe,

And smilest upon the stroke that murders me.

FRIAR LAWRENCE.

O deadly sin, O rude unthankfulness!

Thy fault our law calls death, but the kind Prince,

Taking thy part, hath brush'd aside the law,

And turn'd that black word death to banishment.

This is dear mercy, and thou see'st it not.

ROMEO.

'Tis torture, and not mercy. Heaven is here

Where Juliet lives, and every cat and dog,

And little mouse, every unworthy thing,

Live here in heaven and may look on her,

But Romeo may not. More validity,

More honourable state, more courtship lives

In carrion flies than Romeo. They may seize

On the white wonder of dear Juliet's hand,

And steal immortal blessing from her lips,

Who, even in pure and vestal modesty

Still blush, as thinking their own kisses sin.

But Romeo may not, he is banished.

This may flies do, when I from this must fly.

They are free men but I am banished.

And say'st thou yet that exile is not death?

Hadst thou no poison mix'd, no sharp-ground knife,

No sudden mean of death, though ne'er so mean,

But banished to kill me? Banished?

O Friar, the damned use that word in hell.

Howlings attends it. How hast thou the heart,

Being a divine, a ghostly confessor,

A sin-absolver, and my friend profess'd,

To mangle me with that word banished?

FRIAR LAWRENCE.

Thou fond mad man, hear me speak a little,

ROMEO.

O, thou wilt speak again of banishment.

FRIAR LAWRENCE.

I'll give thee armour to keep off that word,

Adversity's sweet milk, philosophy,

To comfort thee, though thou art banished.

ROMEO.

Yet banished? Hang up philosophy.

Unless philosophy can make a Juliet,

Displant a town, reverse a Prince's doom,

It helps not, it prevails not, talk no more.

FRIAR LAWRENCE.

O, then I see that mad men have no ears.

ROMEO.

How should they, when that wise men have no eyes?

FRIAR LAWRENCE.

Let me dispute with thee of thy estate.

ROMEO.

Thou canst not speak of that thou dost not feel.

Wert thou as young as I, Juliet thy love,

An hour but married, Tybalt murdered,

Doting like me, and like me banished,

Then mightst thou speak, then mightst thou tear thy hair,

And fall upon the ground as I do now,

Taking the measure of an unmade grave.

[Knocking within.]

FRIAR LAWRENCE.

Arise; one knocks. Good Romeo, hide thyself.

ROMEO.

Not I, unless the breath of heartsick groans

Mist-like infold me from the search of eyes.

[Knocking.]

FRIAR LAWRENCE.

Hark, how they knock!—Who's there?—Romeo, arise,

Thou wilt be taken.—Stay awhile.—Stand up.

[Knocking.]

Run to my study.—By-and-by.—God's will,

What simpleness is this.—I come, I come.

[Knocking.]

Who knocks so hard? Whence come you, what's your will?

NURSE.

[Within.] Let me come in, and you shall know my errand.

I come from Lady Juliet.

FRIAR LAWRENCE.

Welcome then.

Enter Nurse.

NURSE.

O holy Friar, O, tell me, holy Friar,

Where is my lady's lord, where's Romeo?

271

FRIAR LAWRENCE.

There on the ground, with his own tears made drunk.

NURSE.

O, he is even in my mistress' case.

Just in her case! O woeful sympathy!

Piteous predicament. Even so lies she,

Blubbering and weeping, weeping and blubbering.

Stand up, stand up; stand, and you be a man.

For Juliet's sake, for her sake, rise and stand.

Why should you fall into so deep an O?

ROMEO.

Nurse.

NURSE.

Ah sir, ah sir, death's the end of all.

ROMEO.

Spakest thou of Juliet? How is it with her?

Doth not she think me an old murderer,

Now I have stain'd the childhood of our joy

With blood remov'd but little from her own?

Where is she? And how doth she? And what says

My conceal'd lady to our cancell'd love?

NURSE.

O, she says nothing, sir, but weeps and weeps;

And now falls on her bed, and then starts up,

And Tybalt calls, and then on Romeo cries,

And then down falls again.

ROMEO.

As if that name,

Shot from the deadly level of a gun,

Did murder her, as that name's cursed hand

Murder'd her kinsman. O, tell me, Friar, tell me,

In what vile part of this anatomy

Doth my name lodge? Tell me, that I may sack

The hateful mansion.

[Drawing his sword.]

FRIAR LAWRENCE.

Hold thy desperate hand.

Art thou a man? Thy form cries out thou art.

Thy tears are womanish, thy wild acts denote

The unreasonable fury of a beast.

Unseemly woman in a seeming man,

And ill-beseeming beast in seeming both!

Thou hast amaz'd me. By my holy order,

I thought thy disposition better temper'd.

Hast thou slain Tybalt? Wilt thou slay thyself?

And slay thy lady, that in thy life lives,

By doing damned hate upon thyself?

Why rail'st thou on thy birth, the heaven and earth?

Since birth, and heaven and earth, all three do meet

In thee at once; which thou at once wouldst lose.

Fie, fie, thou sham'st thy shape, thy love, thy wit,

Which, like a usurer, abound'st in all,

And usest none in that true use indeed

Which should bedeck thy shape, thy love, thy wit.

Thy noble shape is but a form of wax,

Digressing from the valour of a man;

Thy dear love sworn but hollow perjury,

Killing that love which thou hast vow'd to cherish;

Thy wit, that ornament to shape and love,

Misshapen in the conduct of them both,

Like powder in a skilless soldier's flask,

Is set afire by thine own ignorance,

And thou dismember'd with thine own defence.

What, rouse thee, man. Thy Juliet is alive,

For whose dear sake thou wast but lately dead.

There art thou happy. Tybalt would kill thee,

But thou slew'st Tybalt; there art thou happy.

The law that threaten'd death becomes thy friend,

And turns it to exile; there art thou happy.

A pack of blessings light upon thy back;

Happiness courts thee in her best array;

But like a misshaped and sullen wench,

Thou putt'st up thy Fortune and thy love.

Take heed, take heed, for such die miserable.

Go, get thee to thy love as was decreed,

Ascend her chamber, hence and comfort her.

But look thou stay not till the watch be set,

For then thou canst not pass to Mantua;

Where thou shalt live till we can find a time

To blaze your marriage, reconcile your friends,

Beg pardon of the Prince, and call thee back

With twenty hundred thousand times more joy

Than thou went'st forth in lamentation.

Go before, Nurse. Commend me to thy lady,

And bid her hasten all the house to bed,

Which heavy sorrow makes them apt unto.

Romeo is coming.

NURSE.

O Lord, I could have stay'd here all the night

To hear good counsel. O, what learning is!

My lord, I'll tell my lady you will come.

ROMEO.

Do so, and bid my sweet prepare to chide.

NURSE.

Here sir, a ring she bid me give you, sir.

Hie you, make haste, for it grows very late.

[Exit.]

ROMEO.

How well my comfort is reviv'd by this.

FRIAR LAWRENCE.

Go hence, good night, and here stands all your state:

Either be gone before the watch be set,

Or by the break of day disguis'd from hence.

Sojourn in Mantua. I'll find out your man,

And he shall signify from time to time

Every good hap to you that chances here.

Give me thy hand; 'tis late; farewell; good night.

ROMEO.

But that a joy past joy calls out on me,

It were a grief so brief to part with thee.

Farewell.

[Exeunt.]

SCENE IV. A Room in Capulet's House.

Enter Capulet, Lady Capulet and Paris.

CAPULET.

Things have fallen out, sir, so unluckily

That we have had no time to move our daughter.

Look you, she lov'd her kinsman Tybalt dearly,

And so did I. Well, we were born to die.

'Tis very late; she'll not come down tonight.

I promise you, but for your company,

I would have been abed an hour ago.

PARIS.

These times of woe afford no tune to woo.

Madam, good night. Commend me to your daughter.

LADY CAPULET.

I will, and know her mind early tomorrow;

Tonight she's mew'd up to her heaviness.

CAPULET.

Sir Paris, I will make a desperate tender

Of my child's love. I think she will be rul'd

In all respects by me; nay more, I doubt it not.

Wife, go you to her ere you go to bed,

Acquaint her here of my son Paris' love,

And bid her, mark you me, on Wednesday next,

But, soft, what day is this?

PARIS.

Monday, my lord.

CAPULET.

Monday! Ha, ha! Well, Wednesday is too soon,

A Thursday let it be; a Thursday, tell her,

She shall be married to this noble earl.

Will you be ready? Do you like this haste?

We'll keep no great ado,—a friend or two,

For, hark you, Tybalt being slain so late,

It may be thought we held him carelessly,

Being our kinsman, if we revel much.

Therefore we'll have some half a dozen friends,

And there an end. But what say you to Thursday?

PARIS.

My lord, I would that Thursday were tomorrow.

CAPULET.

Well, get you gone. A Thursday be it then.

Go you to Juliet ere you go to bed,

Prepare her, wife, against this wedding day.

Farewell, my lord.—Light to my chamber, ho!

Afore me, it is so very very late that we

May call it early by and by. Good night.

[Exeunt.]

SCENE V. An open Gallery to Juliet's Chamber, overlooking the Garden.

Enter Romeo and Juliet.

JULIET.

Wilt thou be gone? It is not yet near day.

It was the nightingale, and not the lark,

That pierc'd the fearful hollow of thine ear;

Nightly she sings on yond pomegranate tree.

Believe me, love, it was the nightingale.

ROMEO.

It was the lark, the herald of the morn,

No nightingale. Look, love, what envious streaks

Do lace the severing clouds in yonder east.

Night's candles are burnt out, and jocund day

Stands tiptoe on the misty mountain tops.

I must be gone and live, or stay and die.

JULIET.

Yond light is not daylight, I know it, I.

It is some meteor that the sun exhales

To be to thee this night a torchbearer

And light thee on thy way to Mantua.

Therefore stay yet, thou need'st not to be gone.

ROMEO.

Let me be ta'en, let me be put to death,

I am content, so thou wilt have it so.

I'll say yon grey is not the morning's eye,

'Tis but the pale reflex of Cynthia's brow.

Nor that is not the lark whose notes do beat

The vaulty heaven so high above our heads.

I have more care to stay than will to go.

Come, death, and welcome. Juliet wills it so.

How is't, my soul? Let's talk. It is not day.

JULIET.

It is, it is! Hie hence, be gone, away.

It is the lark that sings so out of tune,

Straining harsh discords and unpleasing sharps.

Some say the lark makes sweet division;

This doth not so, for she divideth us.

Some say the lark and loathed toad change eyes.

O, now I would they had chang'd voices too,

Since arm from arm that voice doth us affray,

Hunting thee hence with hunt's-up to the day.

O now be gone, more light and light it grows.

ROMEO.

More light and light, more dark and dark our woes.

Enter Nurse.

NURSE.

Madam.

JULIET.

Nurse?

NURSE.

Your lady mother is coming to your chamber.

The day is broke, be wary, look about.

[Exit.]

JULIET.

Then, window, let day in, and let life out.

ROMEO.

Farewell, farewell, one kiss, and I'll descend.

[Descends.]

JULIET.

Art thou gone so? Love, lord, ay husband, friend,

I must hear from thee every day in the hour,

For in a minute there are many days.

O, by this count I shall be much in years

Ere I again behold my Romeo.

ROMEO.

Farewell!

I will omit no opportunity

That may convey my greetings, love, to thee.

JULIET.

O thinkest thou we shall ever meet again?

ROMEO.

I doubt it not, and all these woes shall serve

For sweet discourses in our time to come.

JULIET.

O God! I have an ill-divining soul!

Methinks I see thee, now thou art so low,

As one dead in the bottom of a tomb.

Either my eyesight fails, or thou look'st pale.

ROMEO.

And trust me, love, in my eye so do you.

Dry sorrow drinks our blood. Adieu, adieu.

[Exit below.]

JULIET.

O Fortune, Fortune! All men call thee fickle,

If thou art fickle, what dost thou with him

That is renown'd for faith? Be fickle, Fortune;

For then, I hope thou wilt not keep him long

But send him back.

LADY CAPULET.

[Within.] Ho, daughter, are you up?

JULIET.

Who is't that calls? Is it my lady mother?

Is she not down so late, or up so early?

What unaccustom'd cause procures her hither?

Enter Lady Capulet.

LADY CAPULET.

Why, how now, Juliet?

JULIET.

Madam, I am not well.

LADY CAPULET.

Evermore weeping for your cousin's death?

What, wilt thou wash him from his grave with tears?

And if thou couldst, thou couldst not make him live.

Therefore have done: some grief shows much of love,

But much of grief shows still some want of wit.

JULIET.

Yet let me weep for such a feeling loss.

LADY CAPULET.

So shall you feel the loss, but not the friend

Which you weep for.

JULIET.

Feeling so the loss,

I cannot choose but ever weep the friend.

LADY CAPULET.

Well, girl, thou weep'st not so much for his death

As that the villain lives which slaughter'd him.

JULIET.

What villain, madam?

LADY CAPULET.

That same villain Romeo.

JULIET.

Villain and he be many miles asunder.

God pardon him. I do, with all my heart.

And yet no man like he doth grieve my heart.

LADY CAPULET.

That is because the traitor murderer lives.

JULIET.

Ay madam, from the reach of these my hands.

Would none but I might venge my cousin's death.

LADY CAPULET.

We will have vengeance for it, fear thou not.

Then weep no more. I'll send to one in Mantua,

Where that same banish'd runagate doth live,

Shall give him such an unaccustom'd dram

That he shall soon keep Tybalt company:

And then I hope thou wilt be satisfied.

JULIET.

Indeed I never shall be satisfied

With Romeo till I behold him—dead—

Is my poor heart so for a kinsman vex'd.

Madam, if you could find out but a man

To bear a poison, I would temper it,

That Romeo should upon receipt thereof,

Soon sleep in quiet. O, how my heart abhors

To hear him nam'd, and cannot come to him,

To wreak the love I bore my cousin

Upon his body that hath slaughter'd him.

LADY CAPULET.

Find thou the means, and I'll find such a man.

But now I'll tell thee joyful tidings, girl.

JULIET.

And joy comes well in such a needy time.

What are they, I beseech your ladyship?

LADY CAPULET.

Well, well, thou hast a careful father, child;

One who to put thee from thy heaviness,

Hath sorted out a sudden day of joy,

That thou expects not, nor I look'd not for.

JULIET.

Madam, in happy time, what day is that?

LADY CAPULET.

Marry, my child, early next Thursday morn

The gallant, young, and noble gentleman,

The County Paris, at Saint Peter's Church,

Shall happily make thee there a joyful bride.

JULIET.

Now by Saint Peter's Church, and Peter too,

He shall not make me there a joyful bride.

I wonder at this haste, that I must wed

Ere he that should be husband comes to woo.

I pray you tell my lord and father, madam,

I will not marry yet; and when I do, I swear

It shall be Romeo, whom you know I hate,

Rather than Paris. These are news indeed.

LADY CAPULET.

Here comes your father, tell him so yourself,

And see how he will take it at your hands.

Enter Capulet and Nurse.

CAPULET.

When the sun sets, the air doth drizzle dew;

But for the sunset of my brother's son

It rains downright.

How now? A conduit, girl? What, still in tears?

Evermore showering? In one little body

Thou counterfeits a bark, a sea, a wind.

For still thy eyes, which I may call the sea,

Do ebb and flow with tears; the bark thy body is,

Sailing in this salt flood, the winds, thy sighs,

Who raging with thy tears and they with them,

Without a sudden calm will overset

Thy tempest-tossed body. How now, wife?

Have you deliver'd to her our decree?

LADY CAPULET.

Ay, sir; but she will none, she gives you thanks.

I would the fool were married to her grave.

CAPULET.

Soft. Take me with you, take me with you, wife.

How, will she none? Doth she not give us thanks?

Is she not proud? Doth she not count her blest,

Unworthy as she is, that we have wrought

So worthy a gentleman to be her bridegroom?

JULIET.

Not proud you have, but thankful that you have.

Proud can I never be of what I hate;

But thankful even for hate that is meant love.

CAPULET.

How now, how now, chopp'd logic? What is this?

Proud, and, I thank you, and I thank you not;

And yet not proud. Mistress minion you,

Thank me no thankings, nor proud me no prouds,

But fettle your fine joints 'gainst Thursday next

To go with Paris to Saint Peter's Church,

Or I will drag thee on a hurdle thither.

Out, you green-sickness carrion! Out, you baggage!

You tallow-face!

LADY CAPULET.

Fie, fie! What, are you mad?

JULIET.

Good father, I beseech you on my knees,

Hear me with patience but to speak a word.

CAPULET.

Hang thee young baggage, disobedient wretch!

I tell thee what,—get thee to church a Thursday,

Or never after look me in the face.

Speak not, reply not, do not answer me.

My fingers itch. Wife, we scarce thought us blest

That God had lent us but this only child;

But now I see this one is one too much,

And that we have a curse in having her.

Out on her, hilding.

NURSE.

God in heaven bless her.

You are to blame, my lord, to rate her so.

CAPULET.

And why, my lady wisdom? Hold your tongue,

Good prudence; smatter with your gossips, go.

NURSE.

I speak no treason.

CAPULET.

O God ye good-en!

NURSE.

May not one speak?

CAPULET.

Peace, you mumbling fool!

Utter your gravity o'er a gossip's bowl,

For here we need it not.

LADY CAPULET.

You are too hot.

CAPULET.

God's bread, it makes me mad!

Day, night, hour, ride, time, work, play,

Alone, in company, still my care hath been

To have her match'd, and having now provided

A gentleman of noble parentage,

Of fair demesnes, youthful, and nobly allied,

Stuff'd, as they say, with honourable parts,

Proportion'd as one's thought would wish a man,

And then to have a wretched puling fool,

A whining mammet, in her fortune's tender,

To answer, 'I'll not wed, I cannot love,

I am too young, I pray you pardon me.'

But, and you will not wed, I'll pardon you.

Graze where you will, you shall not house with me.

Look to't, think on't, I do not use to jest.

Thursday is near; lay hand on heart, advise.

And you be mine, I'll give you to my friend;

And you be not, hang, beg, starve, die in the streets,

For by my soul, I'll ne'er acknowledge thee,

Nor what is mine shall never do thee good.

Trust to't, bethink you, I'll not be forsworn.

[Exit.]

JULIET.

Is there no pity sitting in the clouds,

That sees into the bottom of my grief?

O sweet my mother, cast me not away,

Delay this marriage for a month, a week,

Or, if you do not, make the bridal bed

In that dim monument where Tybalt lies.

LADY CAPULET.

Talk not to me, for I'll not speak a word.

Do as thou wilt, for I have done with thee.

[Exit.]

JULIET.

O God! O Nurse, how shall this be prevented?

My husband is on earth, my faith in heaven.

How shall that faith return again to earth,

Unless that husband send it me from heaven

By leaving earth? Comfort me, counsel me.

Alack, alack, that heaven should practise stratagems

Upon so soft a subject as myself.

What say'st thou? Hast thou not a word of joy?

Some comfort, Nurse.

NURSE.

Faith, here it is.

Romeo is banished; and all the world to nothing

That he dares ne'er come back to challenge you.

Or if he do, it needs must be by stealth.

Then, since the case so stands as now it doth,

I think it best you married with the County.

O, he's a lovely gentleman.

Romeo's a dishclout to him. An eagle, madam,

Hath not so green, so quick, so fair an eye

As Paris hath. Beshrew my very heart,

I think you are happy in this second match,

For it excels your first: or if it did not,

Your first is dead, or 'twere as good he were,

As living here and you no use of him.

JULIET.

Speakest thou from thy heart?

NURSE.

And from my soul too,

Or else beshrew them both.

JULIET.

Amen.

NURSE.

What?

JULIET.

Well, thou hast comforted me marvellous much.

Go in, and tell my lady I am gone,

Having displeas'd my father, to Lawrence' cell,

To make confession and to be absolv'd.

NURSE.

Marry, I will; and this is wisely done.

[Exit.]

JULIET.

Ancient damnation! O most wicked fiend!

Is it more sin to wish me thus forsworn,

Or to dispraise my lord with that same tongue

Which she hath prais'd him with above compare

So many thousand times? Go, counsellor.

Thou and my bosom henceforth shall be twain.

I'll to the Friar to know his remedy.

If all else fail, myself have power to die.

[Exit.]

ACT IV

SCENE I. Friar Lawrence's Cell.

Enter Friar Lawrence and Paris.

FRIAR LAWRENCE.

On Thursday, sir? The time is very short.

PARIS.

My father Capulet will have it so;

And I am nothing slow to slack his haste.

FRIAR LAWRENCE.

You say you do not know the lady's mind.

Uneven is the course; I like it not.

PARIS.

Immoderately she weeps for Tybalt's death,

And therefore have I little talk'd of love;

For Venus smiles not in a house of tears.

Now, sir, her father counts it dangerous

That she do give her sorrow so much sway;

And in his wisdom, hastes our marriage,

To stop the inundation of her tears,

Which, too much minded by herself alone,

May be put from her by society.

Now do you know the reason of this haste.

FRIAR LAWRENCE.

[Aside.] I would I knew not why it should be slow'd.—

Look, sir, here comes the lady toward my cell.

Enter Juliet.

PARIS.

Happily met, my lady and my wife!

JULIET.

That may be, sir, when I may be a wife.

PARIS.

That may be, must be, love, on Thursday next.

JULIET.

What must be shall be.

FRIAR LAWRENCE.

That's a certain text.

PARIS.

Come you to make confession to this father?

JULIET.

To answer that, I should confess to you.

PARIS.

Do not deny to him that you love me.

JULIET.

I will confess to you that I love him.

PARIS.

So will ye, I am sure, that you love me.

JULIET.

If I do so, it will be of more price,

Being spoke behind your back than to your face.

PARIS.

Poor soul, thy face is much abus'd with tears.

JULIET.

The tears have got small victory by that;

For it was bad enough before their spite.

PARIS.

Thou wrong'st it more than tears with that report.

JULIET.

That is no slander, sir, which is a truth,

And what I spake, I spake it to my face.

PARIS.

Thy face is mine, and thou hast slander'd it.

JULIET.

It may be so, for it is not mine own.

Are you at leisure, holy father, now,

Or shall I come to you at evening mass?

FRIAR LAWRENCE.

My leisure serves me, pensive daughter, now.—

My lord, we must entreat the time alone.

PARIS.

God shield I should disturb devotion!—

Juliet, on Thursday early will I rouse ye,

Till then, adieu; and keep this holy kiss.

[Exit.]

JULIET.

O shut the door, and when thou hast done so,

Come weep with me, past hope, past cure, past help!

FRIAR LAWRENCE.

O Juliet, I already know thy grief;

It strains me past the compass of my wits.

I hear thou must, and nothing may prorogue it,

On Thursday next be married to this County.

JULIET.

Tell me not, Friar, that thou hear'st of this,

Unless thou tell me how I may prevent it.

If in thy wisdom, thou canst give no help,

Do thou but call my resolution wise,

And with this knife I'll help it presently.

God join'd my heart and Romeo's, thou our hands;

And ere this hand, by thee to Romeo's seal'd,

Shall be the label to another deed,

Or my true heart with treacherous revolt

Turn to another, this shall slay them both.

Therefore, out of thy long-experienc'd time,

Give me some present counsel, or behold

'Twixt my extremes and me this bloody knife

Shall play the empire, arbitrating that

Which the commission of thy years and art

Could to no issue of true honour bring.

Be not so long to speak. I long to die,

If what thou speak'st speak not of remedy.

FRIAR LAWRENCE.

Hold, daughter. I do spy a kind of hope,

Which craves as desperate an execution

As that is desperate which we would prevent.

If, rather than to marry County Paris

Thou hast the strength of will to slay thyself,

Then is it likely thou wilt undertake

A thing like death to chide away this shame,

That cop'st with death himself to scape from it.

And if thou dar'st, I'll give thee remedy.

JULIET.

O, bid me leap, rather than marry Paris,

From off the battlements of yonder tower,

Or walk in thievish ways, or bid me lurk

Where serpents are. Chain me with roaring bears;

Or hide me nightly in a charnel-house,

O'er-cover'd quite with dead men's rattling bones,

With reeky shanks and yellow chapless skulls.

Or bid me go into a new-made grave,

And hide me with a dead man in his shroud;

Things that, to hear them told, have made me tremble,

And I will do it without fear or doubt,

To live an unstain'd wife to my sweet love.

FRIAR LAWRENCE.

Hold then. Go home, be merry, give consent

To marry Paris. Wednesday is tomorrow;

Tomorrow night look that thou lie alone,

Let not thy Nurse lie with thee in thy chamber.

Take thou this vial, being then in bed,

And this distilled liquor drink thou off,

When presently through all thy veins shall run

A cold and drowsy humour; for no pulse

Shall keep his native progress, but surcease.

No warmth, no breath shall testify thou livest,

The roses in thy lips and cheeks shall fade

To paly ashes; thy eyes' windows fall,

Like death when he shuts up the day of life.

Each part depriv'd of supple government,

Shall stiff and stark and cold appear like death.

And in this borrow'd likeness of shrunk death

Thou shalt continue two and forty hours,

And then awake as from a pleasant sleep.

Now when the bridegroom in the morning comes

To rouse thee from thy bed, there art thou dead.

Then as the manner of our country is,

In thy best robes, uncover'd, on the bier,

Thou shalt be borne to that same ancient vault

Where all the kindred of the Capulets lie.

In the meantime, against thou shalt awake,

Shall Romeo by my letters know our drift,

And hither shall he come, and he and I

Will watch thy waking, and that very night

Shall Romeo bear thee hence to Mantua.

And this shall free thee from this present shame,

If no inconstant toy nor womanish fear

Abate thy valour in the acting it.

JULIET.

Give me, give me! O tell not me of fear!

FRIAR LAWRENCE.

Hold; get you gone, be strong and prosperous

In this resolve. I'll send a friar with speed

To Mantua, with my letters to thy lord.

JULIET.

Love give me strength, and strength shall help afford.

Farewell, dear father.

[Exeunt.]

SCENE II. Hall in Capulet's House.

Enter Capulet, Lady Capulet, Nurse and Servants.

CAPULET.

So many guests invite as here are writ.

[Exit first Servant.]

Sirrah, go hire me twenty cunning cooks.

SECOND SERVANT.

You shall have none ill, sir; for I'll try if they can lick their fingers.

CAPULET.

How canst thou try them so?

SECOND SERVANT.

Marry, sir, 'tis an ill cook that cannot lick his own fingers; therefore he that cannot lick his fingers goes not with me.

CAPULET.

Go, begone.

[Exit second Servant.]

We shall be much unfurnish'd for this time.

What, is my daughter gone to Friar Lawrence?

NURSE.

Ay, forsooth.

CAPULET.

Well, he may chance to do some good on her.

A peevish self-will'd harlotry it is.

Enter Juliet.

NURSE.

See where she comes from shrift with merry look.

CAPULET.

How now, my headstrong. Where have you been gadding?

JULIET.

Where I have learnt me to repent the sin

Of disobedient opposition

To you and your behests; and am enjoin'd

By holy Lawrence to fall prostrate here,

To beg your pardon. Pardon, I beseech you.

Henceforward I am ever rul'd by you.

CAPULET.

Send for the County, go tell him of this.

I'll have this knot knit up tomorrow morning.

JULIET.

I met the youthful lord at Lawrence' cell,

And gave him what becomed love I might,

Not stepping o'er the bounds of modesty.

CAPULET.

Why, I am glad on't. This is well. Stand up.

This is as't should be. Let me see the County.

Ay, marry. Go, I say, and fetch him hither.

Now afore God, this reverend holy Friar,

All our whole city is much bound to him.

JULIET.

Nurse, will you go with me into my closet,

To help me sort such needful ornaments

As you think fit to furnish me tomorrow?

LADY CAPULET.

No, not till Thursday. There is time enough.

CAPULET.

Go, Nurse, go with her. We'll to church tomorrow.

[Exeunt Juliet and Nurse.]

LADY CAPULET.

We shall be short in our provision,

'Tis now near night.

CAPULET.

Tush, I will stir about,

And all things shall be well, I warrant thee, wife.

Go thou to Juliet, help to deck up her.

I'll not to bed tonight, let me alone.

I'll play the housewife for this once.—What, ho!—

They are all forth: well, I will walk myself

To County Paris, to prepare him up

Against tomorrow. My heart is wondrous light

Since this same wayward girl is so reclaim'd.

[Exeunt.]

SCENE III. Juliet's Chamber.

Enter Juliet and Nurse.

JULIET.

Ay, those attires are best. But, gentle Nurse,

I pray thee leave me to myself tonight;

For I have need of many orisons

To move the heavens to smile upon my state,

Which, well thou know'st, is cross and full of sin.

Enter Lady Capulet.

LADY CAPULET.

What, are you busy, ho? Need you my help?

JULIET.

No, madam; we have cull'd such necessaries

As are behoveful for our state tomorrow.

So please you, let me now be left alone,

And let the nurse this night sit up with you,

For I am sure you have your hands full all

In this so sudden business.

LADY CAPULET.

Good night.

Get thee to bed and rest, for thou hast need.

[Exeunt Lady Capulet and Nurse.]

JULIET.

Farewell. God knows when we shall meet again.

I have a faint cold fear thrills through my veins

That almost freezes up the heat of life.

I'll call them back again to comfort me.

Nurse!—What should she do here?

My dismal scene I needs must act alone.

Come, vial.

What if this mixture do not work at all?

Shall I be married then tomorrow morning?

No, No! This shall forbid it. Lie thou there.

[Laying down her dagger.]

What if it be a poison, which the Friar

Subtly hath minister'd to have me dead,

Lest in this marriage he should be dishonour'd,

Because he married me before to Romeo?

I fear it is. And yet methinks it should not,

For he hath still been tried a holy man.

How if, when I am laid into the tomb,

I wake before the time that Romeo

Come to redeem me? There's a fearful point!

Shall I not then be stifled in the vault,

To whose foul mouth no healthsome air breathes in,

And there die strangled ere my Romeo comes?

Or, if I live, is it not very like,

The horrible conceit of death and night,

Together with the terror of the place,

As in a vault, an ancient receptacle,

Where for this many hundred years the bones

Of all my buried ancestors are pack'd,

Where bloody Tybalt, yet but green in earth,

Lies festering in his shroud; where, as they say,

At some hours in the night spirits resort—

Alack, alack, is it not like that I,

So early waking, what with loathsome smells,

And shrieks like mandrakes torn out of the earth,

That living mortals, hearing them, run mad.

O, if I wake, shall I not be distraught,

Environed with all these hideous fears,

And madly play with my forefathers' joints?

And pluck the mangled Tybalt from his shroud?

And, in this rage, with some great kinsman's bone,

As with a club, dash out my desperate brains?

O look, methinks I see my cousin's ghost

Seeking out Romeo that did spit his body

Upon a rapier's point. Stay, Tybalt, stay!

Romeo, Romeo, Romeo, here's drink! I drink to thee.

[Throws herself on the bed.]

SCENE IV. Hall in Capulet's House.

Enter Lady Capulet and Nurse.

LADY CAPULET.

Hold, take these keys and fetch more spices, Nurse.

NURSE.

They call for dates and quinces in the pastry.

Enter Capulet.

CAPULET.

Come, stir, stir, stir! The second cock hath crow'd,

The curfew bell hath rung, 'tis three o'clock.

Look to the bak'd meats, good Angelica;

Spare not for cost.

NURSE.

Go, you cot-quean, go,

Get you to bed; faith, you'll be sick tomorrow

For this night's watching.

CAPULET.

No, not a whit. What! I have watch'd ere now

All night for lesser cause, and ne'er been sick.

LADY CAPULET.

Ay, you have been a mouse-hunt in your time;

But I will watch you from such watching now.

[Exeunt Lady Capulet and Nurse.]

CAPULET.

A jealous-hood, a jealous-hood!

Enter Servants, with spits, logs and baskets.

Now, fellow, what's there?

FIRST SERVANT.

Things for the cook, sir; but I know not what.

CAPULET.

Make haste, make haste.

[Exit First Servant.]

—Sirrah, fetch drier logs.

Call Peter, he will show thee where they are.

SECOND SERVANT.

I have a head, sir, that will find out logs

And never trouble Peter for the matter.

[Exit.]

CAPULET.

Mass and well said; a merry whoreson, ha.

Thou shalt be loggerhead.—Good faith, 'tis day.

The County will be here with music straight,

For so he said he would. I hear him near.

[Play music.]

Nurse! Wife! What, ho! What, Nurse, I say!

Re-enter Nurse.

Go waken Juliet, go and trim her up.

I'll go and chat with Paris. Hie, make haste,

Make haste; the bridegroom he is come already.

Make haste I say.

[Exeunt.]

SCENE V. Juliet's Chamber; Juliet on the bed.

Enter Nurse.

NURSE.

Mistress! What, mistress! Juliet! Fast, I warrant her, she.

Why, lamb, why, lady, fie, you slug-abed!

Why, love, I say! Madam! Sweetheart! Why, bride!

What, not a word? You take your pennyworths now.

Sleep for a week; for the next night, I warrant,

The County Paris hath set up his rest

That you shall rest but little. God forgive me!

Marry and amen. How sound is she asleep!

I needs must wake her. Madam, madam, madam!

Ay, let the County take you in your bed,

He'll fright you up, i'faith. Will it not be?

What, dress'd, and in your clothes, and down again?

I must needs wake you. Lady! Lady! Lady!

Alas, alas! Help, help! My lady's dead!

O, well-a-day that ever I was born.

Some aqua vitae, ho! My lord! My lady!

Enter Lady Capulet.

LADY CAPULET.

What noise is here?

NURSE.

O lamentable day!

LADY CAPULET.

What is the matter?

NURSE.

Look, look! O heavy day!

LADY CAPULET.

O me, O me! My child, my only life.

Revive, look up, or I will die with thee.

Help, help! Call help.

Enter Capulet.

CAPULET.

For shame, bring Juliet forth, her lord is come.

NURSE.

She's dead, deceas'd, she's dead; alack the day!

LADY CAPULET.

Alack the day, she's dead, she's dead, she's dead!

CAPULET.

Ha! Let me see her. Out alas! She's cold,

Her blood is settled and her joints are stiff.

Life and these lips have long been separated.

Death lies on her like an untimely frost

Upon the sweetest flower of all the field.

NURSE.

O lamentable day!

LADY CAPULET.

O woful time!

CAPULET.

Death, that hath ta'en her hence to make me wail,

Ties up my tongue and will not let me speak.

Enter Friar Lawrence and Paris with Musicians.

FRIAR LAWRENCE.

Come, is the bride ready to go to church?

CAPULET.

Ready to go, but never to return.

O son, the night before thy wedding day

Hath death lain with thy bride. There she lies,

Flower as she was, deflowered by him.

Death is my son-in-law, death is my heir;

My daughter he hath wedded. I will die.

And leave him all; life, living, all is death's.

PARIS.

Have I thought long to see this morning's face,

And doth it give me such a sight as this?

LADY CAPULET.

Accurs'd, unhappy, wretched, hateful day.

Most miserable hour that e'er time saw

In lasting labour of his pilgrimage.

But one, poor one, one poor and loving child,

But one thing to rejoice and solace in,

And cruel death hath catch'd it from my sight.

NURSE.

O woe! O woeful, woeful, woeful day.

Most lamentable day, most woeful day

That ever, ever, I did yet behold!

O day, O day, O day, O hateful day.

Never was seen so black a day as this.

O woeful day, O woeful day.

PARIS.

Beguil'd, divorced, wronged, spited, slain.

Most detestable death, by thee beguil'd,

By cruel, cruel thee quite overthrown.

O love! O life! Not life, but love in death!

CAPULET.

Despis'd, distressed, hated, martyr'd, kill'd.

Uncomfortable time, why cam'st thou now

To murder, murder our solemnity?

O child! O child! My soul, and not my child,

Dead art thou. Alack, my child is dead,

And with my child my joys are buried.

FRIAR LAWRENCE.

Peace, ho, for shame. Confusion's cure lives not

In these confusions. Heaven and yourself

Had part in this fair maid, now heaven hath all,

And all the better is it for the maid.

Your part in her you could not keep from death,

But heaven keeps his part in eternal life.

The most you sought was her promotion,

For 'twas your heaven she should be advanc'd,

And weep ye now, seeing she is advanc'd

Above the clouds, as high as heaven itself?

O, in this love, you love your child so ill

That you run mad, seeing that she is well.

She's not well married that lives married long,

But she's best married that dies married young.

Dry up your tears, and stick your rosemary

On this fair corse, and, as the custom is,

And in her best array bear her to church;

For though fond nature bids us all lament,

Yet nature's tears are reason's merriment.

CAPULET.

All things that we ordained festival

Turn from their office to black funeral:

Our instruments to melancholy bells,

Our wedding cheer to a sad burial feast;

Our solemn hymns to sullen dirges change;

Our bridal flowers serve for a buried corse,

And all things change them to the contrary.

FRIAR LAWRENCE.

Sir, go you in, and, madam, go with him,

And go, Sir Paris, everyone prepare

To follow this fair corse unto her grave.

The heavens do lower upon you for some ill;

Move them no more by crossing their high will.

[Exeunt Capulet, Lady Capulet, Paris and Friar.]

FIRST MUSICIAN.

Faith, we may put up our pipes and be gone.

NURSE.

Honest good fellows, ah, put up, put up,

For well you know this is a pitiful case.

FIRST MUSICIAN.

Ay, by my troth, the case may be amended.

[Exit Nurse.]

Enter Peter.

PETER.

Musicians, O, musicians, 'Heart's ease,' 'Heart's ease', O, and you will have me live, play 'Heart's ease.'

FIRST MUSICIAN.

Why 'Heart's ease'?

PETER.

O musicians, because my heart itself plays 'My heart is full'. O play me some merry dump to comfort me.

FIRST MUSICIAN.

Not a dump we, 'tis no time to play now.

PETER.

You will not then?

FIRST MUSICIAN.

No.

PETER.

I will then give it you soundly.

FIRST MUSICIAN.

What will you give us?

PETER.

No money, on my faith, but the gleek! I will give you the minstrel.

FIRST MUSICIAN.

Then will I give you the serving-creature.

PETER.

Then will I lay the serving-creature's dagger on your pate. I will carry no crotchets. I'll re you, I'll fa you. Do you note me?

FIRST MUSICIAN.

And you re us and fa us, you note us.

SECOND MUSICIAN.

Pray you put up your dagger, and put out your wit.

PETER.

Then have at you with my wit. I will dry-beat you with an iron wit, and put up my iron dagger. Answer me like men.

'When griping griefs the heart doth wound,

And doleful dumps the mind oppress,

Then music with her silver sound'—

Why 'silver sound'? Why 'music with her silver sound'? What say you, Simon Catling?

FIRST MUSICIAN.

Marry, sir, because silver hath a sweet sound.

PETER.

Prates. What say you, Hugh Rebeck?

SECOND MUSICIAN.

I say 'silver sound' because musicians sound for silver.

PETER.

Prates too! What say you, James Soundpost?

THIRD MUSICIAN.

Faith, I know not what to say.

PETER.

O, I cry you mercy, you are the singer. I will say for you. It is 'music with her silver sound' because musicians have no gold for sounding.

'Then music with her silver sound

With speedy help doth lend redress.'

[Exit.]

FIRST MUSICIAN.

What a pestilent knave is this same!

SECOND MUSICIAN.

Hang him, Jack. Come, we'll in here, tarry for the mourners, and stay dinner.

[Exeunt.]

ACT V

SCENE I. Mantua. A Street.

Enter Romeo.

ROMEO.

If I may trust the flattering eye of sleep,

My dreams presage some joyful news at hand.

My bosom's lord sits lightly in his throne;

And all this day an unaccustom'd spirit

Lifts me above the ground with cheerful thoughts.

I dreamt my lady came and found me dead,—

Strange dream, that gives a dead man leave to think!—

And breath'd such life with kisses in my lips,

That I reviv'd, and was an emperor.

Ah me, how sweet is love itself possess'd,

When but love's shadows are so rich in joy.

Enter Balthasar.

News from Verona! How now, Balthasar?

Dost thou not bring me letters from the Friar?

How doth my lady? Is my father well?

How fares my Juliet? That I ask again;

For nothing can be ill if she be well.

BALTHASAR.

Then she is well, and nothing can be ill.

Her body sleeps in Capel's monument,

And her immortal part with angels lives.

I saw her laid low in her kindred's vault,

And presently took post to tell it you.

O pardon me for bringing these ill news,

Since you did leave it for my office, sir.

ROMEO.

Is it even so? Then I defy you, stars!

Thou know'st my lodging. Get me ink and paper,

And hire post-horses. I will hence tonight.

BALTHASAR.

I do beseech you sir, have patience.

Your looks are pale and wild, and do import

Some misadventure.

ROMEO.

Tush, thou art deceiv'd.

Leave me, and do the thing I bid thee do.

Hast thou no letters to me from the Friar?

BALTHASAR.

No, my good lord.

ROMEO.

No matter. Get thee gone,

And hire those horses. I'll be with thee straight.

[Exit Balthasar.]

Well, Juliet, I will lie with thee tonight.

Let's see for means. O mischief thou art swift

To enter in the thoughts of desperate men.

I do remember an apothecary,—

And hereabouts he dwells,—which late I noted

In tatter'd weeds, with overwhelming brows,

Culling of simples, meagre were his looks,

Sharp misery had worn him to the bones;

And in his needy shop a tortoise hung,

An alligator stuff'd, and other skins

Of ill-shaped fishes; and about his shelves

A beggarly account of empty boxes,

Green earthen pots, bladders, and musty seeds,

Remnants of packthread, and old cakes of roses

Were thinly scatter'd, to make up a show.

Noting this penury, to myself I said,

And if a man did need a poison now,

Whose sale is present death in Mantua,

Here lives a caitiff wretch would sell it him.

O, this same thought did but forerun my need,

And this same needy man must sell it me.

As I remember, this should be the house.

Being holiday, the beggar's shop is shut.

What, ho! Apothecary!

Enter Apothecary.

APOTHECARY.

Who calls so loud?

ROMEO.

Come hither, man. I see that thou art poor.

Hold, there is forty ducats. Let me have

A dram of poison, such soon-speeding gear

As will disperse itself through all the veins,

That the life-weary taker may fall dead,

And that the trunk may be discharg'd of breath

As violently as hasty powder fir'd

Doth hurry from the fatal cannon's womb.

APOTHECARY.

Such mortal drugs I have, but Mantua's law

Is death to any he that utters them.

ROMEO.

Art thou so bare and full of wretchedness,

And fear'st to die? Famine is in thy cheeks,

Need and oppression starveth in thine eyes,

Contempt and beggary hangs upon thy back.

The world is not thy friend, nor the world's law;

The world affords no law to make thee rich;

Then be not poor, but break it and take this.

APOTHECARY.

My poverty, but not my will consents.

ROMEO.

I pay thy poverty, and not thy will.

APOTHECARY.

Put this in any liquid thing you will

And drink it off; and, if you had the strength

Of twenty men, it would despatch you straight.

ROMEO.

There is thy gold, worse poison to men's souls,

Doing more murder in this loathsome world

Than these poor compounds that thou mayst not sell.

I sell thee poison, thou hast sold me none.

Farewell, buy food, and get thyself in flesh.

Come, cordial and not poison, go with me

To Juliet's grave, for there must I use thee.

[Exeunt.]

SCENE II. Friar Lawrence's Cell.

Enter Friar John.

FRIAR JOHN.

Holy Franciscan Friar! Brother, ho!

Enter Friar Lawrence.

FRIAR LAWRENCE.

This same should be the voice of Friar John.

Welcome from Mantua. What says Romeo?

Or, if his mind be writ, give me his letter.

FRIAR JOHN.

Going to find a barefoot brother out,

One of our order, to associate me,

Here in this city visiting the sick,

And finding him, the searchers of the town,

Suspecting that we both were in a house

Where the infectious pestilence did reign,

Seal'd up the doors, and would not let us forth,

So that my speed to Mantua there was stay'd.

FRIAR LAWRENCE.

Who bare my letter then to Romeo?

FRIAR JOHN.

I could not send it,—here it is again,—

Nor get a messenger to bring it thee,

So fearful were they of infection.

FRIAR LAWRENCE.

Unhappy fortune! By my brotherhood,

The letter was not nice, but full of charge,

Of dear import, and the neglecting it

May do much danger. Friar John, go hence,

Get me an iron crow and bring it straight

Unto my cell.

FRIAR JOHN.

Brother, I'll go and bring it thee.

[Exit.]

FRIAR LAWRENCE.

Now must I to the monument alone.

Within this three hours will fair Juliet wake.

She will beshrew me much that Romeo

Hath had no notice of these accidents;

But I will write again to Mantua,

And keep her at my cell till Romeo come.

Poor living corse, clos'd in a dead man's tomb.

[Exit.]

SCENE III. A churchyard; in it a Monument belonging to the Capulets.

Enter Paris, and his Page bearing flowers and a torch.

PARIS.

Give me thy torch, boy. Hence and stand aloof.

Yet put it out, for I would not be seen.

Under yond yew tree lay thee all along,

Holding thy ear close to the hollow ground;

So shall no foot upon the churchyard tread,

Being loose, unfirm, with digging up of graves,

But thou shalt hear it. Whistle then to me,

As signal that thou hear'st something approach.

Give me those flowers. Do as I bid thee, go.

PAGE.

[Aside.] I am almost afraid to stand alone

Here in the churchyard; yet I will adventure.

[Retires.]

PARIS.

Sweet flower, with flowers thy bridal bed I strew.

O woe, thy canopy is dust and stones,

Which with sweet water nightly I will dew,

Or wanting that, with tears distill'd by moans.

The obsequies that I for thee will keep,

Nightly shall be to strew thy grave and weep.

[The Page whistles.]

The boy gives warning something doth approach.

What cursed foot wanders this way tonight,

To cross my obsequies and true love's rite?

What, with a torch! Muffle me, night, awhile.

[Retires.]

Enter Romeo and Balthasar with a torch, mattock, &c.

ROMEO.

Give me that mattock and the wrenching iron.

Hold, take this letter; early in the morning

See thou deliver it to my lord and father.

Give me the light; upon thy life I charge thee,

Whate'er thou hear'st or seest, stand all aloof

And do not interrupt me in my course.

Why I descend into this bed of death

Is partly to behold my lady's face,

But chiefly to take thence from her dead finger

A precious ring, a ring that I must use

In dear employment. Therefore hence, be gone.

But if thou jealous dost return to pry

In what I further shall intend to do,

By heaven I will tear thee joint by joint,

And strew this hungry churchyard with thy limbs.

The time and my intents are savage-wild;

More fierce and more inexorable far

Than empty tigers or the roaring sea.

BALTHASAR.

I will be gone, sir, and not trouble you.

ROMEO.

So shalt thou show me friendship. Take thou that.

Live, and be prosperous, and farewell, good fellow.

BALTHASAR.

For all this same, I'll hide me hereabout.

His looks I fear, and his intents I doubt.

[Retires]

ROMEO.

Thou detestable maw, thou womb of death,

Gorg'd with the dearest morsel of the earth,

Thus I enforce thy rotten jaws to open,

[Breaking open the door of the monument.]

And in despite, I'll cram thee with more food.

PARIS.

This is that banish'd haughty Montague

That murder'd my love's cousin,—with which grief,

It is supposed, the fair creature died,—

And here is come to do some villanous shame

To the dead bodies. I will apprehend him.

[Advances.]

Stop thy unhallow'd toil, vile Montague.

Can vengeance be pursu'd further than death?

Condemned villain, I do apprehend thee.

Obey, and go with me, for thou must die.

ROMEO.

I must indeed; and therefore came I hither.

Good gentle youth, tempt not a desperate man.

Fly hence and leave me. Think upon these gone;

Let them affright thee. I beseech thee, youth,

Put not another sin upon my head

By urging me to fury. O be gone.

By heaven I love thee better than myself;

For I come hither arm'd against myself.

Stay not, be gone, live, and hereafter say,

A madman's mercy bid thee run away.

PARIS.

I do defy thy conjuration,

And apprehend thee for a felon here.

ROMEO.

Wilt thou provoke me? Then have at thee, boy!

[They fight.]

PAGE.

O lord, they fight! I will go call the watch.

[Exit.]

PARIS.

O, I am slain! [Falls.] If thou be merciful,

Open the tomb, lay me with Juliet.

[Dies.]

ROMEO.

In faith, I will. Let me peruse this face.

Mercutio's kinsman, noble County Paris!

What said my man, when my betossed soul

Did not attend him as we rode? I think

He told me Paris should have married Juliet.

Said he not so? Or did I dream it so?

Or am I mad, hearing him talk of Juliet,

To think it was so? O, give me thy hand,

One writ with me in sour misfortune's book.

I'll bury thee in a triumphant grave.

A grave? O no, a lantern, slaught'red youth,

For here lies Juliet, and her beauty makes

This vault a feasting presence full of light.

Death, lie thou there, by a dead man interr'd.

[Laying Paris in the monument.]

How oft when men are at the point of death

Have they been merry! Which their keepers call

331

A lightning before death. O, how may I

Call this a lightning? O my love, my wife,

Death that hath suck'd the honey of thy breath,

Hath had no power yet upon thy beauty.

Thou art not conquer'd. Beauty's ensign yet

Is crimson in thy lips and in thy cheeks,

And death's pale flag is not advanced there.

Tybalt, liest thou there in thy bloody sheet?

O, what more favour can I do to thee

Than with that hand that cut thy youth in twain

To sunder his that was thine enemy?

Forgive me, cousin. Ah, dear Juliet,

Why art thou yet so fair? Shall I believe

That unsubstantial death is amorous;

And that the lean abhorred monster keeps

Thee here in dark to be his paramour?

For fear of that I still will stay with thee,

And never from this palace of dim night

Depart again. Here, here will I remain

With worms that are thy chambermaids. O, here

Will I set up my everlasting rest;

And shake the yoke of inauspicious stars

From this world-wearied flesh. Eyes, look your last.

Arms, take your last embrace! And, lips, O you

The doors of breath, seal with a righteous kiss

A dateless bargain to engrossing death.

Come, bitter conduct, come, unsavoury guide.

Thou desperate pilot, now at once run on

The dashing rocks thy sea-sick weary bark.

Here's to my love! [Drinks.] O true apothecary!

Thy drugs are quick. Thus with a kiss I die.

[Dies.]

Enter, at the other end of the Churchyard, Friar Lawrence, with a lantern, crow, and spade.

FRIAR LAWRENCE.

Saint Francis be my speed. How oft tonight

Have my old feet stumbled at graves? Who's there?

Who is it that consorts, so late, the dead?

BALTHASAR.

Here's one, a friend, and one that knows you well.

FRIAR LAWRENCE.

Bliss be upon you. Tell me, good my friend,

What torch is yond that vainly lends his light

To grubs and eyeless skulls? As I discern,

It burneth in the Capels' monument.

BALTHASAR.

It doth so, holy sir, and there's my master,

One that you love.

FRIAR LAWRENCE.

Who is it?

BALTHASAR.

Romeo.

FRIAR LAWRENCE.

How long hath he been there?

BALTHASAR.

Full half an hour.

FRIAR LAWRENCE.

Go with me to the vault.

BALTHASAR.

I dare not, sir;

My master knows not but I am gone hence,

And fearfully did menace me with death

If I did stay to look on his intents.

FRIAR LAWRENCE.

Stay then, I'll go alone. Fear comes upon me.

O, much I fear some ill unlucky thing.

BALTHASAR.

As I did sleep under this yew tree here,

I dreamt my master and another fought,

And that my master slew him.

FRIAR LAWRENCE.

Romeo! [Advances.]

Alack, alack, what blood is this which stains

The stony entrance of this sepulchre?

What mean these masterless and gory swords

To lie discolour'd by this place of peace?

[Enters the monument.]

Romeo! O, pale! Who else? What, Paris too?

And steep'd in blood? Ah what an unkind hour

Is guilty of this lamentable chance?

The lady stirs.

[Juliet wakes and stirs.]

JULIET.

O comfortable Friar, where is my lord?

I do remember well where I should be,

And there I am. Where is my Romeo?

[Noise within.]

FRIAR LAWRENCE.

I hear some noise. Lady, come from that nest

Of death, contagion, and unnatural sleep.

A greater power than we can contradict

Hath thwarted our intents. Come, come away.

Thy husband in thy bosom there lies dead;

And Paris too. Come, I'll dispose of thee

Among a sisterhood of holy nuns.

Stay not to question, for the watch is coming.

Come, go, good Juliet. I dare no longer stay.

JULIET.

Go, get thee hence, for I will not away.

[Exit Friar Lawrence.]

What's here? A cup clos'd in my true love's hand?

Poison, I see, hath been his timeless end.

O churl. Drink all, and left no friendly drop

To help me after? I will kiss thy lips.

Haply some poison yet doth hang on them,

To make me die with a restorative.

[Kisses him.]

Thy lips are warm!

FIRST WATCH.

[Within.] Lead, boy. Which way?

JULIET.

Yea, noise? Then I'll be brief. O happy dagger.

[Snatching Romeo's dagger.]

This is thy sheath. [stabs herself] There rest, and let me die.

[Falls on Romeo's body and dies.]

Enter Watch with the Page of Paris.

PAGE.

This is the place. There, where the torch doth burn.

FIRST WATCH.

The ground is bloody. Search about the churchyard.

Go, some of you, whoe'er you find attach.

[Exeunt some of the Watch.]

Pitiful sight! Here lies the County slain,

And Juliet bleeding, warm, and newly dead,

Who here hath lain this two days buried.

Go tell the Prince; run to the Capulets.

Raise up the Montagues, some others search.

[Exeunt others of the Watch.]

We see the ground whereon these woes do lie,

But the true ground of all these piteous woes

We cannot without circumstance descry.

Re-enter some of the Watch with Balthasar.

SECOND WATCH.

Here's Romeo's man. We found him in the churchyard.

FIRST WATCH.

Hold him in safety till the Prince come hither.

Re-enter others of the Watch with Friar Lawrence.

THIRD WATCH.

Here is a Friar that trembles, sighs, and weeps.

We took this mattock and this spade from him

As he was coming from this churchyard side.

FIRST WATCH.

A great suspicion. Stay the Friar too.

Enter the Prince and Attendants.

PRINCE.

What misadventure is so early up,

That calls our person from our morning's rest?

Enter Capulet, Lady Capulet and others.

CAPULET.

What should it be that they so shriek abroad?

LADY CAPULET.

O the people in the street cry Romeo,

Some Juliet, and some Paris, and all run

With open outcry toward our monument.

PRINCE.

What fear is this which startles in our ears?

FIRST WATCH.

Sovereign, here lies the County Paris slain,

And Romeo dead, and Juliet, dead before,

Warm and new kill'd.

PRINCE.

Search, seek, and know how this foul murder comes.

FIRST WATCH.

Here is a Friar, and slaughter'd Romeo's man,

With instruments upon them fit to open

These dead men's tombs.

CAPULET.

O heaven! O wife, look how our daughter bleeds!

This dagger hath mista'en, for lo, his house

Is empty on the back of Montague,

And it mis-sheathed in my daughter's bosom.

LADY CAPULET.

O me! This sight of death is as a bell

That warns my old age to a sepulchre.

Enter Montague and others.

PRINCE.

Come, Montague, for thou art early up,

To see thy son and heir more early down.

MONTAGUE.

Alas, my liege, my wife is dead tonight.

Grief of my son's exile hath stopp'd her breath.

What further woe conspires against mine age?

PRINCE.

Look, and thou shalt see.

MONTAGUE.

O thou untaught! What manners is in this,

To press before thy father to a grave?

PRINCE.

Seal up the mouth of outrage for a while,

Till we can clear these ambiguities,

And know their spring, their head, their true descent,

And then will I be general of your woes,

And lead you even to death. Meantime forbear,

And let mischance be slave to patience.

Bring forth the parties of suspicion.

FRIAR LAWRENCE.

I am the greatest, able to do least,

Yet most suspected, as the time and place

Doth make against me, of this direful murder.

And here I stand, both to impeach and purge

Myself condemned and myself excus'd.

PRINCE.

Then say at once what thou dost know in this.

FRIAR LAWRENCE.

I will be brief, for my short date of breath

Is not so long as is a tedious tale.

Romeo, there dead, was husband to that Juliet,

And she, there dead, that Romeo's faithful wife.

I married them; and their stol'n marriage day

Was Tybalt's doomsday, whose untimely death

Banish'd the new-made bridegroom from this city;

For whom, and not for Tybalt, Juliet pin'd.

You, to remove that siege of grief from her,

Betroth'd, and would have married her perforce

To County Paris. Then comes she to me,

And with wild looks, bid me devise some means

To rid her from this second marriage,

Or in my cell there would she kill herself.

Then gave I her, so tutored by my art,

A sleeping potion, which so took effect

As I intended, for it wrought on her

The form of death. Meantime I writ to Romeo

That he should hither come as this dire night

To help to take her from her borrow'd grave,

Being the time the potion's force should cease.

But he which bore my letter, Friar John,

Was stay'd by accident; and yesternight

Return'd my letter back. Then all alone

At the prefixed hour of her waking

Came I to take her from her kindred's vault,

Meaning to keep her closely at my cell

Till I conveniently could send to Romeo.

But when I came, some minute ere the time

Of her awaking, here untimely lay

The noble Paris and true Romeo dead.

She wakes; and I entreated her come forth

And bear this work of heaven with patience.

But then a noise did scare me from the tomb;

And she, too desperate, would not go with me,

But, as it seems, did violence on herself.

All this I know; and to the marriage

Her Nurse is privy. And if ought in this

Miscarried by my fault, let my old life

Be sacrific'd, some hour before his time,

Unto the rigour of severest law.

PRINCE.

We still have known thee for a holy man.

Where's Romeo's man? What can he say to this?

BALTHASAR.

I brought my master news of Juliet's death,

And then in post he came from Mantua

To this same place, to this same monument.

This letter he early bid me give his father,

And threaten'd me with death, going in the vault,

If I departed not, and left him there.

PRINCE.

Give me the letter, I will look on it.

Where is the County's Page that rais'd the watch?

Sirrah, what made your master in this place?

PAGE.

He came with flowers to strew his lady's grave,

And bid me stand aloof, and so I did.

Anon comes one with light to ope the tomb,

And by and by my master drew on him,

And then I ran away to call the watch.

PRINCE.

This letter doth make good the Friar's words,

Their course of love, the tidings of her death.

And here he writes that he did buy a poison

Of a poor 'pothecary, and therewithal

Came to this vault to die, and lie with Juliet.

Where be these enemies? Capulet, Montague,

See what a scourge is laid upon your hate,

That heaven finds means to kill your joys with love!

And I, for winking at your discords too,

Have lost a brace of kinsmen. All are punish'd.

CAPULET.

O brother Montague, give me thy hand.

This is my daughter's jointure, for no more

Can I demand.

MONTAGUE.

But I can give thee more,

For I will raise her statue in pure gold,

That whiles Verona by that name is known,

There shall no figure at such rate be set

As that of true and faithful Juliet.

CAPULET.

As rich shall Romeo's by his lady's lie,

Poor sacrifices of our enmity.

PRINCE.

A glooming peace this morning with it brings;

The sun for sorrow will not show his head.

Go hence, to have more talk of these sad things.

Some shall be pardon'd, and some punished,

For never was a story of more woe

Than this of Juliet and her Romeo.

[Exeunt.]

About Author

Shakespeare produced most of his known works between 1589 and 1613. His early plays were primarily comedies and histories and are regarded as some of the best work produced in these genres. Until about 1608, he wrote mainly tragedies, among them Hamlet, Othello, King Lear, and Macbeth, all considered to be among the finest works in the English language. In the last phase of his life, he wrote tragicomedies (also known as romances) and collaborated with other playwrights.

Many of Shakespeare's plays were published in editions of varying quality and accuracy in his lifetime. However, in 1623, two fellow actors and friends of Shakespeare's, John Heminges and Henry Condell, published a more definitive text known as the First Folio, a posthumous collected edition of Shakespeare's dramatic works that included all but two of his plays. The volume was prefaced with a poem by Ben Jonson, in which Jonson presciently hails Shakespeare in a now-famous quote as "not of an age, but for all time".

Throughout the 20th and 21st centuries, Shakespeare's works have been continually adapted and rediscovered by new movements in scholarship and performance. His plays remain popular and are studied, performed, and reinterpreted through various cultural and political contexts around the world.

Early life

William Shakespeare was the son of John Shakespeare, an alderman and a successful glover (glove-maker) originally from Snitterfield, and Mary Arden, the daughter of an affluent landowning farmer. He was born in Stratford-upon-Avon and baptised there on 26 April 1564. His actual date of birth remains unknown, but is traditionally observed on 23 April, Saint George's Day. This date, which can be traced to a mistake made by an 18th-century scholar, has proved appealing to biographers because Shakespeare died on the same date in 1616. He was the third of eight children, and the eldest surviving son.

Although no attendance records for the period survive, most biographers agree that Shakespeare was probably educated at the King's New School in Stratford, a free school chartered in 1553, about a quarter-mile (400 m) from his home. Grammar schools varied in quality during the Elizabethan era, but grammar school curricula were largely similar: the basic Latin text was standardised by royal decree, and the school would have provided an intensive education in grammar based upon Latin classical authors.

At the age of 18, Shakespeare married 26-year-old Anne Hathaway. The consistory court of the Diocese of Worcester issued a marriage licence on 27 November 1582. The next day, two of Hathaway's neighbours posted bonds guaranteeing that no lawful claims impeded the marriage. The ceremony may have been arranged in some haste since the Worcester chancellor allowed the marriage banns to be read once instead of the usual three times, and six months after the marriage Anne gave birth to a daughter, Susanna, baptised 26 May 1583. Twins, son Hamnet and daughter Judith, followed almost two years later and were baptised 2 February 1585. Hamnet died of unknown causes at the age of 11 and was buried 11 August 1596.

After the birth of the twins, Shakespeare left few historical traces until he is mentioned as part of the London theatre scene in 1592. The exception is the appearance of his name in the "complaints bill" of a law case before the Queen's Bench court at Westminster dated Michaelmas Term 1588 and 9 October 1589. Scholars refer to the years between 1585 and 1592 as Shakespeare's "lost years". Biographers attempting to account for this period have reported many apocryphal stories. Nicholas Rowe, Shakespeare's first biographer, recounted a Stratford legend that Shakespeare fled the town for London to escape prosecution for deer poaching in the estate of local squire Thomas Lucy. Shakespeare is also supposed to have taken his revenge on Lucy by writing a scurrilous ballad about him. Another 18th-century story has Shakespeare starting his theatrical career minding the horses of theatre patrons in London. John Aubrey reported that Shakespeare had been a country schoolmaster. Some 20th-century scholars have suggested that Shakespeare may have been employed as a schoolmaster by Alexander

Hoghton of Lancashire, a Catholic landowner who named a certain "William Shakeshafte" in his will. Little evidence substantiates such stories other than hearsay collected after his death, and Shakeshafte was a common name in the Lancashire area.

London and theatrical career

It is not known definitively when Shakespeare began writing, but contemporary allusions and records of performances show that several of his plays were on the London stage by 1592. By then, he was sufficiently known in London to be attacked in print by the playwright Robert Greene in his Groats-Worth of Wit:

... there is an upstart Crow, beautified with our feathers, that with his Tiger's heart wrapped in a Player's hide, supposes he is as well able to bombast out a blank verse as the best of you: and being an absolute Johannes factotum, is in his own conceit the only Shake-scene in a country.

Scholars differ on the exact meaning of Greene's words, but most agree that Greene was accusing Shakespeare of reaching above his rank in trying to match such university-educated writers as Christopher Marlowe, Thomas Nashe, and Greene himself (the so-called "University Wits"). The italicised phrase parodying the line "Oh, tiger's heart wrapped in a woman's hide" from Shakespeare's Henry VI, Part 3, along with the pun "Shake-scene", clearly identify Shakespeare as Greene's target. As used here, Johannes Factotum ("Jack of all trades") refers to a second-rate tinkerer with the work of others, rather than the more common "universal genius".

Greene's attack is the earliest surviving mention of Shakespeare's work in the theatre. Biographers suggest that his career may have begun any time from the mid-1580s to just before Greene's remarks. After 1594, Shakespeare's plays were performed only by the Lord Chamberlain's Men, a company owned by a group of players, including Shakespeare, that soon became the leading playing company in London. After the death of Queen Elizabeth in 1603, the company was awarded a royal patent by the new King James I, and changed its name to the King's Men.

"All the world's a stage,

and all the men and women merely players:

they have their exits and their entrances;

and one man in his time plays many parts ..."

—As You Like It, Act II, Scene 7, 139–142

In 1599, a partnership of members of the company built their own theatre on the south bank of the River Thames, which they named the Globe. In 1608, the partnership also took over the Blackfriars indoor theatre. Extant records of Shakespeare's property purchases and investments indicate that his association with the company made him a wealthy man, and in 1597, he bought the second-largest house in Stratford, New Place, and in 1605, invested in a share of the parish tithes in Stratford.

Some of Shakespeare's plays were published in quarto editions, beginning in 1594, and by 1598, his name had become a selling point and began to appear on the title pages. Shakespeare continued to act in his own and other plays after his success as a playwright. The 1616 edition of Ben Jonson's Works names him on the cast lists for Every Man in His Humour (1598) and Sejanus His Fall (1603). The absence of his name from the 1605 cast list for Jonson's Volpone is taken by some scholars as a sign that his acting career was nearing its end. The First Folio of 1623, however, lists Shakespeare as one of "the Principal Actors in all these Plays", some of which were first staged after Volpone, although we cannot know for certain which roles he played. In 1610, John Davies of Hereford wrote that "good Will" played "kingly" roles. In 1709, Rowe passed down a tradition that Shakespeare played the ghost of Hamlet's father. Later traditions maintain that he also played Adam in As You Like It, and the Chorus in Henry V, though scholars doubt the sources of that information.

Throughout his career, Shakespeare divided his time between London and Stratford. In 1596, the year before he bought New Place as his family home in Stratford, Shakespeare was living in the parish of St. Helen's, Bishopsgate, north of the River Thames. He moved across the river to Southwark by 1599, the same year his company constructed the Globe Theatre there. By 1604, he had moved north of the river again, to an area north of St Paul's Cathedral with many fine houses. There, he rented rooms from a French Huguenot named Christopher Mountjoy, a maker of ladies' wigs and other headgear.

Later years and death

Rowe was the first biographer to record the tradition, repeated by Johnson, that Shakespeare retired to Stratford "some years before his death". He was still working as an actor in London in 1608; in an answer to the sharers' petition in 1635, Cuthbert Burbage stated that after purchasing the lease of the Blackfriars Theatre in 1608 from Henry Evans, the King's Men "placed men players" there, "which were Heminges, Condell, Shakespeare, etc.". However, it is perhaps relevant that the bubonic plague raged in London throughout 1609. The London public playhouses were repeatedly closed during extended outbreaks of the plague (a total of over 60 months closure between May 1603 and February 1610), which meant there was often no acting work. Retirement from all work was uncommon at that time. Shakespeare continued to visit London during the years 1611–1614. In 1612, he was called as a witness in Bellott v. Mountjoy, a court case concerning the marriage settlement of Mountjoy's daughter, Mary. In March 1613, he bought a gatehouse in the former Blackfriars priory; and from November 1614, he was in London for several weeks with his son-in-law, John Hall. After 1610, Shakespeare wrote fewer plays, and none are attributed to him after 1613. His last three plays were collaborations, probably with John Fletcher, who succeeded him as the house playwright of the King's Men.

Shakespeare died on 23 April 1616, at the age of 52. He died within a month of signing his will, a document which he begins by describing himself as being in "perfect health". No extant contemporary source explains how or why he died. Half a century later, John Ward, the vicar of Stratford, wrote in his notebook: "Shakespeare, Drayton, and Ben Jonson had a merry meeting and, it seems, drank too hard, for Shakespeare died of a fever there contracted", not an impossible scenario since Shakespeare knew Jonson and Drayton. Of the tributes from fellow authors, one refers to his relatively sudden death: "We wondered, Shakespeare, that thou went'st so soon / From

351

the world's stage to the grave's tiring room."

He was survived by his wife and two daughters. Susanna had married a physician, John Hall, in 1607, and Judith had married Thomas Quiney, a vintner, two months before Shakespeare's death. Shakespeare signed his last will and testament on 25 March 1616; the following day, his new son-in-law, Thomas Quiney was found guilty of fathering an illegitimate son by Margaret Wheeler, who had died during childbirth. Thomas was ordered by the church court to do public penance, which would have caused much shame and embarrassment for the Shakespeare family.

Shakespeare bequeathed the bulk of his large estate to his elder daughter Susanna under stipulations that she pass it down intact to "the first son of her body". The Quineys had three children, all of whom died without marrying. The Halls had one child, Elizabeth, who married twice but died without children in 1670, ending Shakespeare's direct line. Shakespeare's will scarcely mentions his wife, Anne, who was probably entitled to one-third of his estate automatically. He did make a point, however, of leaving her "my second best bed", a bequest that has led to much speculation. Some scholars see the bequest as an insult to Anne, whereas others believe that the second-best bed would have been the matrimonial bed and therefore rich in significance.

Shakespeare was buried in the chancel of the Holy Trinity Church two days after his death. The epitaph carved into the stone slab covering his grave includes a curse against moving his bones, which was carefully avoided during restoration of the church in 2008:

Good frend for Iesvs sake forbeare,

To digg the dvst encloased heare.

Bleste be Middle English the.svg man Middle English that.svg spares thes stones,

And cvrst be he Middle English that.svg moves my bones.

(Modern spelling: Good friend, for Jesus' sake forbear, / To dig the dust enclosed here. / Blessed be the man that spares these stones, / And cursed be he that moves my bones.)

Some time before 1623, a funerary monument was erected in his memory on the north wall, with a half-effigy of him in the act of writing. Its plaque compares him to Nestor, Socrates, and Virgil. In 1623, in conjunction with the publication of the First Folio, the Droeshout engraving was published.

Shakespeare has been commemorated in many statues and memorials around the world, including funeral monuments in Southwark Cathedral and Poets' Corner in Westminster Abbey.

Plays

Most playwrights of the period typically collaborated with others at some point, and critics agree that Shakespeare did the same, mostly early and late in his career. Some attributions, such as Titus Andronicus and the early history plays, remain controversial while The Two Noble Kinsmen and the lost Cardenio have well-attested contemporary documentation. Textual evidence also supports the view that several of the plays were revised by other writers after their original composition.

The first recorded works of Shakespeare are Richard III and the three parts of Henry VI, written in the early 1590s during a vogue for historical drama. Shakespeare's plays are difficult to date precisely, however, and studies of the texts suggest that Titus Andronicus, The Comedy of Errors, The Taming of the Shrew, and The Two Gentlemen of Verona may also belong to Shakespeare's earliest period. His first histories, which draw heavily on the 1587 edition of Raphael Holinshed's Chronicles of England, Scotland, and Ireland, dramatise the destructive results of weak or corrupt rule and have been interpreted as a justification for the origins of the Tudor dynasty. The early plays were influenced by the works of other Elizabethan dramatists, especially Thomas Kyd and Christopher Marlowe, by the traditions of medieval drama, and by the plays of Seneca. The Comedy of Errors was also based on classical models, but no source for The Taming of the Shrew has been found, though it is related to a separate play of the same name and may have derived from a folk story. Like The Two Gentlemen of Verona, in which two friends appear to approve of rape, the Shrew's story of the taming of a woman's independent spirit by a man sometimes troubles modern critics, directors, and audiences.

Shakespeare's early classical and Italianate comedies, containing tight double plots and precise comic sequences, give way in the mid-1590s to the romantic atmosphere of his most acclaimed comedies. A Midsummer Night's Dream is a witty mixture of romance, fairy magic, and comic lowlife scenes. Shakespeare's next comedy, the equally romantic Merchant of Venice, contains a portrayal of the vengeful Jewish moneylender Shylock, which reflects Elizabethan views but may appear derogatory to modern audiences. The wit and wordplay of Much Ado About Nothing, the charming rural setting of As You Like It, and the lively merrymaking of Twelfth Night complete Shakespeare's sequence of great comedies. After the lyrical Richard II, written almost entirely in verse, Shakespeare introduced prose comedy into the histories of the late 1590s, Henry IV, parts 1 and 2, and Henry V. His characters become more complex and tender as he switches deftly between comic and serious scenes, prose and poetry, and achieves the narrative variety of his mature work. This period begins and ends with two tragedies: Romeo and Juliet, the famous romantic tragedy of sexually charged adolescence, love, and death; and Julius Caesar—based on Sir Thomas North's 1579 translation of Plutarch's Parallel Lives—which introduced a new kind of drama. According to Shakespearean scholar James Shapiro, in Julius Caesar, "the various strands of politics, character, inwardness, contemporary events, even Shakespeare's own reflections on the act of writing, began to infuse each other".

In the early 17th century, Shakespeare wrote the so-called "problem plays" Measure for Measure, Troilus and Cressida, and All's Well That Ends Well and a number of his best known tragedies. Many critics believe that Shakespeare's greatest tragedies represent the peak of his art. The titular hero of one of Shakespeare's greatest tragedies, Hamlet, has probably been discussed more than any other Shakespearean character, especially for his famous soliloquy which begins "To be or not to be; that is the question". Unlike the introverted Hamlet, whose fatal flaw is hesitation, the heroes of the tragedies that followed, Othello and King Lear, are undone by hasty errors of judgement. The plots of Shakespeare's tragedies often hinge on such fatal errors or flaws, which overturn order and destroy the hero and those he loves. In Othello, the villain Iago stokes Othello's sexual jealousy to the point where he murders the innocent wife who loves him. In King Lear, the old king commits the tragic error of giving up his powers, initiating the events which lead to the torture and blinding of the Earl of Gloucester and the murder of Lear's youngest daughter Cordelia. According to the critic Frank Kermode, "the play-offers neither its good characters nor its audience any relief from its cruelty". In Macbeth, the shortest and most compressed of Shakespeare's tragedies, uncontrollable ambition incites Macbeth and his wife, Lady Macbeth, to murder the rightful king and usurp the throne until their own guilt destroys them in turn. In this play, Shakespeare adds a supernatural element to the tragic structure. His last major tragedies, Antony and Cleopatra and Coriolanus, contain some of Shakespeare's finest poetry and were considered his most successful tragedies by the poet and critic T.S. Eliot.

In his final period, Shakespeare turned to romance or tragicomedy and completed three more major plays: Cymbeline, The Winter's Tale, and The Tempest, as well as the collaboration, Pericles, Prince of Tyre. Less bleak than the tragedies, these four plays are graver in tone than the comedies of the 1590s, but they end with reconciliation and the forgiveness of potentially tragic errors. Some commentators have seen this change in mood as evidence of a more serene view of life on Shakespeare's part, but it may merely reflect the theatrical fashion of the day. Shakespeare collaborated on two further surviving plays, Henry VIII and The Two Noble Kinsmen, probably with John Fletcher.

Performances

It is not clear for which companies Shakespeare wrote his early plays. The title page of the 1594 edition of Titus Andronicus reveals that the play had been acted by three different troupes. After the plagues of 1592–3, Shakespeare's plays were performed by his own company at The Theatre and the Curtain in Shoreditch, north of the Thames. Londoners flocked there to see the first part of Henry IV, Leonard Digges recording, "Let but Falstaff come, Hal, Poins, the rest ... and you scarce shall have a room". When the company found themselves in dispute with their landlord, they pulled The

Theatre down and used the timbers to construct the Globe Theatre, the first playhouse built by actors for actors, on the south bank of the Thames at Southwark. The Globe opened in autumn 1599, with Julius Caesar one of the first plays staged. Most of Shakespeare's greatest post-1599 plays were written for the Globe, including Hamlet, Othello, and King Lear.

After the Lord Chamberlain's Men were renamed the King's Men in 1603, they entered a special relationship with the new King James. Although the performance records are patchy, the King's Men performed seven of Shakespeare's plays at court between 1 November 1604, and 31 October 1605, including two performances of The Merchant of Venice. After 1608, they performed at the indoor Blackfriars Theatre during the winter and the Globe during the summer. The indoor setting, combined with the Jacobean fashion for lavishly staged masques, allowed Shakespeare to introduce more elaborate stage devices. In Cymbeline, for example, Jupiter descends "in thunder and lightning, sitting upon an eagle: he throws a thunderbolt. The ghosts fall on their knees."

The actors in Shakespeare's company included the famous Richard Burbage, William Kempe, Henry Condell and John Heminges. Burbage played the leading role in the first performances of many of Shakespeare's plays, including Richard III, Hamlet, Othello, and King Lear. The popular comic actor Will Kempe played the servant Peter in Romeo and Juliet and Dogberry in Much Ado About Nothing, among other characters. He was replaced around 1600 by Robert Armin, who played roles such as Touchstone in As You Like It and the fool in King Lear. In 1613, Sir Henry Wotton recorded that Henry VIII "was set forth with many extraordinary circumstances of pomp and ceremony". On 29 June, however, a cannon set fire to the thatch of the Globe and burned the theatre to the ground, an event which pinpoints the date of a Shakespeare play with rare precision.

Textual sources

In 1623, John Heminges and Henry Condell, two of Shakespeare's friends from the King's Men, published the First Folio, a collected edition of Shakespeare's plays. It contained 36 texts, including 18 printed for the

356

first time. Many of the plays had already appeared in quarto versions—flimsy books made from sheets of paper folded twice to make four leaves. No evidence suggests that Shakespeare approved these editions, which the First Folio describes as "stol'n and surreptitious copies". Nor did Shakespeare plan or expect his works to survive in any form at all; those works likely would have faded into oblivion but for his friends' spontaneous idea, after his death, to create and publish the First Folio.

Alfred Pollard termed some of the pre-1623 versions as "bad quartos" because of their adapted, paraphrased or garbled texts, which may in places have been reconstructed from memory. Where several versions of a play survive, each differs from the other. The differences may stem from copying or printing errors, from notes by actors or audience members, or from Shakespeare's own papers. In some cases, for example, Hamlet, Troilus and Cressida, and Othello, Shakespeare could have revised the texts between the quarto and folio editions. In the case of King Lear, however, while most modern editions do conflate them, the 1623 folio version is so different from the 1608 quarto that the Oxford Shakespeare prints them both, arguing that they cannot be conflated without confusion.

Influence from neighbours in London

Ten years of research by Geoffrey Marsh (museum director) of the Victoria and Albert Museum in London may have shown that Shakespeare got many of the ideas and information for his plays, from his neighbours that he lived near in London in the late 1590s.

Geoffrey Marsh found the site of Shakespeare's house in St Helen's Church, Bishopsgate parish, at the corner of St.Helen's churchyard and Bishopsgate Street, north of the churchyard, from the records of the Leathersellers Company. Many wealthy and notable people (including Sir John Spencer and Dr. Edward Jorden and Dr. Peter Turner), with connections across Europe, lived near Shakespeare.

Poems

In 1593 and 1594, when the theatres were closed because of plague,

Shakespeare published two narrative poems on sexual themes, Venus and Adonis and The Rape of Lucrece. He dedicated them to Henry Wriothesley, Earl of Southampton. In Venus and Adonis, an innocent Adonis rejects the sexual advances of Venus; while in The Rape of Lucrece, the virtuous wife Lucrece is raped by the lustful Tarquin. Influenced by Ovid's Metamorphoses, the poems show the guilt and moral confusion that result from uncontrolled lust. Both proved popular and were often reprinted during Shakespeare's lifetime. A third narrative poem, A Lover's Complaint, in which a young woman laments her seduction by a persuasive suitor, was printed in the first edition of the Sonnets in 1609. Most scholars now accept that Shakespeare wrote A Lover's Complaint. Critics consider that its fine qualities are marred by leaden effects. The Phoenix and the Turtle, printed in Robert Chester's 1601 Love's Martyr, mourns the deaths of the legendary phoenix and his lover, the faithful turtle dove. In 1599, two early drafts of sonnets 138 and 144 appeared in The Passionate Pilgrim, published under Shakespeare's name but without his permission.

Sonnets

Published in 1609, the Sonnets were the last of Shakespeare's non-dramatic works to be printed. Scholars are not certain when each of the 154 sonnets was composed, but evidence suggests that Shakespeare wrote sonnets throughout his career for a private readership. Even before the two unauthorised sonnets appeared in The Passionate Pilgrim in 1599, Francis Meres had referred in 1598 to Shakespeare's "sugred Sonnets among his private friends". Few analysts believe that the published collection follows Shakespeare's intended sequence. He seems to have planned two contrasting series: one about uncontrollable lust for a married woman of dark complexion (the "dark lady"), and one about conflicted love for a fair young man (the "fair youth"). It remains unclear if these figures represent real individuals, or if the authorial "I" who addresses them represents Shakespeare himself, though Wordsworth believed that with the sonnets "Shakespeare unlocked his heart".

"Shall I compare thee to a summer's day?

Thou art more lovely and more temperate ..."

—Lines from Shakespeare's Sonnet 18.

The 1609 edition was dedicated to a "Mr. W.H.", credited as "the only begetter" of the poems. It is not known whether this was written by Shakespeare himself or by the publisher, Thomas Thorpe, whose initials appear at the foot of the dedication page; nor is it known who Mr. W.H. was, despite numerous theories, or whether Shakespeare even authorised the publication. Critics praise the Sonnets as a profound meditation on the nature of love, sexual passion, procreation, death, and time.

Style

Shakespeare's first plays were written in the conventional style of the day. He wrote them in a stylised language that does not always spring naturally from the needs of the characters or the drama. The poetry depends on extended, sometimes elaborate metaphors and conceits, and the language is often rhetorical—written for actors to declaim rather than speak. The grand speeches in Titus Andronicus, in the view of some critics, often hold up the action, for example; and the verse in The Two Gentlemen of Verona has been described as stilted.

However, Shakespeare soon began to adapt the traditional styles to his own purposes. The opening soliloquy of Richard III has its roots in the self-declaration of Vice in medieval drama. At the same time, Richard's vivid self-awareness looks forward to the soliloquies of Shakespeare's mature plays. No single play marks a change from the traditional to the freer style. Shakespeare combined the two throughout his career, with Romeo and Juliet perhaps the best example of the mixing of the styles. By the time of Romeo and Juliet, Richard II, and A Midsummer Night's Dream in the mid-1590s, Shakespeare had begun to write a more natural poetry. He increasingly tuned his metaphors and images to the needs of the drama itself.

Shakespeare's standard poetic form was blank verse, composed in iambic pentameter. In practice, this meant that his verse was usually unrhymed and consisted of ten syllables to a line, spoken with a stress on every second syllable. The blank verse of his early plays is quite different from that of his later ones. It is often beautiful, but its sentences tend to start, pause, and finish at the end of lines, with the risk of monotony. Once Shakespeare mastered traditional blank verse, he began to interrupt and vary its flow. This technique releases the new power and flexibility of the poetry in plays such as Julius Caesar and Hamlet. Shakespeare uses it, for example, to convey the turmoil in Hamlet's mind:

> Sir, in my heart there was a kind of fighting
>
> That would not let me sleep. Methought I lay
>
> Worse than the mutines in the bilboes. Rashly—
>
> And prais'd be rashness for it—let us know
>
> Our indiscretion sometimes serves us well ...
>
> —Hamlet, Act 5, Scene 2, 4–8

After Hamlet, Shakespeare varied his poetic style further, particularly in the more emotional passages of the late tragedies. The literary critic A. C. Bradley described this style as "more concentrated, rapid, varied, and, in construction, less regular, not seldom twisted or elliptical". In the last phase of his career, Shakespeare adopted many techniques to achieve these effects. These included run-on lines, irregular pauses and stops, and extreme variations in sentence structure and length. In Macbeth, for example, the language darts from one unrelated metaphor or simile to another: "was the hope drunk/ Wherein you dressed yourself?" (1.7.35–38); "... pity, like a naked new-born babe/ Striding the blast, or heaven's cherubim, hors'd/ Upon the sightless couriers of the air ..." (1.7.21–25). The listener is challenged to complete the sense. The late romances, with their shifts in time and surprising turns of plot, inspired a last poetic style in which long and short sentences are set against one another, clauses are piled up, subject and object are reversed, and words are omitted, creating an effect of spontaneity.

Shakespeare combined poetic genius with a practical sense of the theatre. Like all playwrights of the time, he dramatised stories from sources such as Plutarch and Holinshed. He reshaped each plot to create several centres of interest and to show as many sides of a narrative to the audience as possible. This strength of design ensures that a Shakespeare play can survive translation, cutting and wide interpretation without loss to its core drama. As Shakespeare's mastery grew, he gave his characters clearer and more varied motivations and distinctive patterns of speech. He preserved aspects of his earlier style in the later plays, however. In Shakespeare's late romances, he deliberately returned to a more artificial style, which emphasised the illusion of theatre.

Influence

Shakespeare's work has made a lasting impression on later theatre and literature. In particular, he expanded the dramatic potential of characterisation, plot, language, and genre. Until Romeo and Juliet, for example, romance had not been viewed as a worthy topic for tragedy. Soliloquies had been used mainly to convey information about characters or events, but Shakespeare used them to explore characters' minds. His work heavily influenced later poetry. The Romantic poets attempted to revive Shakespearean verse drama, though with little success. Critic George Steiner described all English verse dramas from Coleridge to Tennyson as "feeble variations on Shakespearean themes."

Shakespeare influenced novelists such as Thomas Hardy, William Faulkner, and Charles Dickens. The American novelist Herman Melville's soliloquies owe much to Shakespeare; his Captain Ahab in Moby-Dick is a classic tragic hero, inspired by King Lear. Scholars have identified 20,000 pieces of music linked to Shakespeare's works. These include three operas by Giuseppe Verdi, Macbeth, Otello and Falstaff, whose critical standing compares with that of the source plays. Shakespeare has also inspired many painters, including the Romantics and the Pre-Raphaelites. The Swiss Romantic artist Henry Fuseli, a friend of William Blake, even translated Macbeth into German. The psychoanalyst Sigmund Freud drew on Shakespearean psychology, in particular, that of Hamlet, for his theories of human nature.

In Shakespeare's day, English grammar, spelling, and pronunciation were less standardised than they are now, and his use of language helped shape modern English. Samuel Johnson quoted him more often than any other author in his A Dictionary of the English Language, the first serious work of its type. Expressions such as "with bated breath" (Merchant of Venice) and "a foregone conclusion" (Othello) have found their way into everyday English speech.

Works

Classification of the plays

Shakespeare's works include the 36 plays printed in the First Folio of 1623, listed according to their folio classification as comedies, histories, and tragedies. Two plays not included in the First Folio, The Two Noble Kinsmen and Pericles, Prince of Tyre, are now accepted as part of the canon, with today's scholars agreeing that Shakespeare made major contributions to the writing of both. No Shakespearean poems were included in the First Folio.

In the late 19th century, Edward Dowden classified four of the late comedies as romances, and though many scholars prefer to call them tragicomedies, Dowden's term is often used. In 1896, Frederick S. Boas coined the term "problem plays" to describe four plays: All's Well That Ends Well, Measure for Measure, Troilus and Cressida, and Hamlet. "Dramas as singular in theme and temper cannot be strictly called comedies or tragedies", he wrote. "We may, therefore, borrow a convenient phrase from the theatre of today and class them together as Shakespeare's problem plays." The term, much debated and sometimes applied to other plays, remains in use, though Hamlet is definitively classed as a tragedy. (Source: Wikipedia)